BestMasters

Springer awards "BestMasters" to the best application-oriented master's theses, which were completed at renowned chairs of economic sciences in Germany, Austria and Switzerland in 2013.

The works received highest marks and were recommended for publication by supervisors. As a rule, they show a high degree of application orientation and deal with current issues from different fields of economics.

The series addresses practitioners as well as scientists and offers guidance for early stage researchers.

Anja Brumme

Wind Energy Deployment and the Relevance of Rare Earths

An Economic Analysis

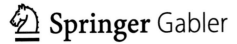

Anja Brumme
Technische Universität Chemnitz
Chemnitz, Germany

ISBN 978-3-658-04912-6   ISBN 978-3-658-04913-3 (eBook)
DOI 10.1007/978-3-658-04913-3

The Deutsche Nationalbibliothek lists this publication in the Deutsche Nationalbibliografie; detailed bibliographic data are available in the Internet at http://dnb.d-nb.de.

Library of Congress Control Number: 2014930983

Springer Gabler

Printed on acid-free paper

Springer Gabler is a brand of Springer DE.
Springer DE is part of Springer Science+Business Media.
www.springer-gabler.de

Praise for
Critical materials for wind power: The relevance of rare elements for wind turbines
by Anja Brumme

This book is an excellent and carefully written contribution to one of the most severe problems of mankind, the issue of climate change. In this frame the long run substitution of renewable energy for fossil energy is discussed, in particular by taking wind power as a special case. What might not be commonly known and is rarely analyzed is the fact that the availability of rare earth elements is crucial for the construction of wind power plants. The study, hence, provides a long run analysis of the inefficiency of the markets for rare earth elements by identifying various market failures. Moreover, some modes of capturing the rare earth side condition which could be implemented in climate change assessment models like the one by the Potsdam Institute are proposed. Mrs. Brumme's work is a fine example for an economics master thesis, originally submitted to the Department of Economics of the University of Technology, Chemnitz, and, most remarkably, carried out in cooperation with the Potsdam Institute in the frame of an internship.

Thomas Kuhn

Acknowledgements

In addition to the supervisors, Prof. Dr. Thomas Kuhn (Chemnitz University of Technology) and Dr. Helga Weisz (Potsdam Institute for Climate Impact Research, Research Domain "Climate Impacts and Vulnerabilities"), the author wants to thank Eva Schmid (Potsdam Institute for Climate Impact Research, Research Domain "Sustainable Solutions") and Dr. Omar Feraboli (Chemnitz University of Technology) for their support and valuable advice.

Contents

List of Figures

List of Tables

List of Abbreviations

Al	aluminium
Aug.	August
B	boron
BGR	Bundesanstalt für Geowissenschaften und Rohstoffe (Federal Institute for Geosciences and Natural Resources)
BMU	Bundesministerium für Umwelt, Naturschutz und Reaktorsicherheit (Federal Ministry for the Environment, Nature Conservation and Nuclear Safety)
BMWi	Bundesministerium für Wirtschaft und Technologie (German Federal Ministry of Economics and Technology)
BWE	Bundesverband WindEnergie e.V. (German WindEnergy Association)
C	Celsius
Cd	cadmium
Ce	cerium
CES	constant elasticity of substitution
cf.	confer (compare)
chap.	chapter
CIS	Commonwealth of Independent States (former Soviet Union)
Co	cobalt
Co.	company
CO_2	carbon dioxide
Cu	copper
d	day
DD	direct drive
Dec.	December
Dena	Deutsche Energie-Agentur (German Energy Agency)
DFIG	doubly-fed induction generator
Dy	dysprosium
EC	European Commission
ed.	edited; edition
EEA	European Environment Agency
e.g.	exempli gratia (for example)
EJ	exajoule
Er	erbium

et al.	et alii (and others)
etc.	et cetera (and so forth)
ETP	Energy Technology Perspectives
Eu	europium
EU	European Union
EWEA	European Wind Energy Association
Fe	iron
Gd	gadolinium
GDP	gross domestic product
GJ	gigajoule
GW	gigawatt
GWEC	Global Wind Energy Council
h	hour
HHI	Herfindahl-Hirschman Index
Ho	holmium
HS	high speed
i.e.	id est (that is)
IEA	International Energy Agency
Inc.	Incorporation
IPCC	Intergovernmental Panel on Climate Change
IT	information technology
Jan.	January
Jun.	June
kg	kilogram
km	kilometer
kt	kiloton
kW	kilowatt
kWh	kilowatt hour
La	lanthanum
LCD	liquid crystal display
LCOE	levelised cost of electricity
Lu	lutetium
m	meter
MBtu	million British thermal units
MS	medium speed
MW	megawatt
MWh	megawatt hour
n.a.	not available
n.d.	no date
Nd	neodymium
Ni	nickel
Nov.	November

NYSERDA	New York State Energy Research and Development Authority
Oct.	October
OECD	Organisation for Economic Cooperation and Development
p.	page
Pb	lead
Pm	promethium
PM	permanent magnet
PMG	permanent magnet generator
pp.	pages
ppm	parts per million
Pr	praseodymium
RE	rare earth
REE	rare earth element
REM	rare earth metal
ReMIND	name of an integrated assessment model
REN21	Renewable Energy Policy Network for the 21st Century
REO	rare earth oxide
s	second
SAR	Special Administrative Region
Sc	scandium
Sept.	September
Sm	samarium
SRREN	Special Report on Renewable Energy Sources and Climate Change Mitigation
t	metric ton
Tb	terbium
tech. rep.	technical report
Tm	thulium
TV	television
TWh	terawatt hour
UNEP	United Nations Environment Programme
URL	uniform resource locator
US	United States
USA	United States of America
USDE	United States Department of Energy
UV	ultraviolet
WBGU	Wissenschaftlicher Beirat der Bundesregierung Globale Umweltveränderungen (German Advisory Council on Global Change)
WTO	World Trade Organization
WWEA	World Wind Energy Association
Y	yttrium

Yb	ytterbium
yr	year
Zn	zinc

List of Symbols

a	recovery rate in the recycling process
b	share parameter in the natural resource demand function
B	intertemporal trade balance
c	marginal cost
C	consumption
D	demand
E	primary energy carrier index
G	composite final good index
G_F	energy system costs for fuel
G_I	investment into the energy system
G_F	energy system operation and maintenance costs
i	iteration step index
I	investment
j	index for the goods traded
J	physical scarcity indicator
K	choke price
L	population; labour force
M	import
p	price
P	production
q	quantity
Q	emission permits index
r	region index
S	natural resource stock
t	time index
T	end of time horizon
U	utility
w	welfare weight
W	global welfare
X	export
Y	GDP
ζ	pure rate of time preference
ρ	interest rate
σ	elasticity of substitution

1 Introduction

Within the spectrum of renewable energy sources, wind power plays an outstanding role. It has been exhibiting enormous growth rates of about 27% annually since 2005, resulting in a doubling of cumulative global capacity in less than three years (REN21 2010). By the end of 2010, 197 GW have been installed altogether (WWEA 2011). In contrast to alternative renewable energy technologies, wind power is already competitive with fossil fuel-fired electricity generation if onshore sites with high wind speeds are regarded (Arvizu et al. 2011; EWEA 2009; Herbert et al. 2007). Moreover, an estimate of life-cycle impacts on air, water and land by OECD and IEA (2010a) yielded exclusively positive findings for wind power. Power generation impacts on air and water were also judged positive, only power generation impacts on land were categorised "variable/uncertain". Out of the nine electricity production technologies analysed, wind power also turned out to emit the least amount of CO_2. Similar results have been obtained for example by Jacobson (2009) and EC (2003).

However, those studies usually do not include co-impacts from plant construction or manufacturing.[1] The fact that wind turbine construction employs input materials whose availability is assessed to be critical (USDE 2010), combined with the soaring deployment of wind power plants, points to a potential problem that has received little attention in literature so far. Whereas the scarcity of natural resources utilised as fossil fuels has been studied extensively, corresponding shortages of power plant construction materials have widely been disregarded.

In order to shed light on the issue of natural resource scarcities affecting wind power deployment, this thesis proceeds as follows. Chapter 2 provides an overview of the technical background of wind power, determining requirements of critical natural resources. As rare earth elements are identified as the most critical input material, a detailed market analysis follows in Chapter 3. Chapter 4 then extends the time horizon to the future deployment of wind power plants and the resulting consequences for rare earth demand. Chapter 5 presents two options for introducing rare earth demand of wind power technologies into the global integrated assessment model ReMIND-R. Finally, Chapter 6 concludes the thesis by summarising the main findings and identifying scope for further research.

---

[1]The OECD and IEA (2010a) study explicitly excludes these effects. The other papers do not state where exactly the limits of their analyses are.

2 Classification of wind power technologies

Literature offers many possibilities to classify wind power technologies, for example with respect to their size (Hennicke et al. 2010), structural shape (Hau 2008), or tower concepts (Neumann et al. 2002). Due to the space restrictions of a master's thesis, it has to be determined which differentiations to cover here. As the focus of this work lies on natural resource restrictions, the categorisation has to be chosen accordingly. Hence, in Section 2.1, several studies are reviewed in order to find out which materials are required for the construction of wind power plants and which of them may become critical in the foreseeable future.

Based on the results from Section 2.1, the subsequent section deals with different generator concepts, as it turns out that these contain the most critical natural resources, namely rare earth elements.

The most obvious alternative, however, is to contrast onshore with offshore wind power, which is done in Section 2.3. Material requirements are slightly different among the two, justifying a deeper look at the topic.

2.1 Requirements of critical natural resources

For assessing the criticality of natural resources for wind power plants, the analysis proceeds in three steps. In the first step, the term "criticality" is defined. Secondly, material requirements for wind power plants are listed. Finally, in the third step, studies are cited that identify critical materials among them, so a conclusion can be drawn concerning what natural resources have to be focused on in the following.

Regarding the definition of "criticality", there is a widespread consensus in literature (see for example EC (2010); Fischedick (2010); USDE (2010)) that the materials under consideration must have the following properties:

- high economic importance

- supply or environmental risk

When considering these two aspects, it makes sense to provide a market analysis of critical materials, covering both demand (i.e. the first point) and supply (to represent the second point), which is done in Chapter 3. Demand-side aspects can further be subdivided into relevance of the natural resource for certain technologies and impracticality of substitution, whereas at the supply side, insufficient stocks, low recycling rates, or high dependencies on single extracting countries contribute to criticality (EC 2010; Fischedick 2010). Additional threats may arise if those extracting countries lack political and/or economic stability (EC 2008).

There are only a few studies listing material requirements of wind power plants in detail; they can primarily be found in the life cycle analysis literature. Among them, the most extensive ones are Jacobson and Delucchi (2011), Ardente et al. (2008), Martínez et al. (2009), Schleisner (2000), Kleijn and Voet (2010) and Weinzettel et al. (2009). Although all of these studies with the exception of Jacobson and Delucchi (2011) provide tangible data of material usage, it has to be kept in mind that these are only exemplified for specific types of wind turbines. Ardente et al. (2008) refer to a windfarm located in Italy, consisting of turbines with a power of 660 kW each. Martínez et al. (2009) derive their analysis from a 2 MW power plant within a Spanish wind farm. Schleisner (2000) presents results for an onshore and an offshore wind farm in Denmark.[1] Kleijn and Voet (2010) list the material use of an 800 kW onshore and a 2 MW offshore turbine. Weinzettel et al. (2009) investigate a 5 MW offshore floating wind power plant by a Norwegian company.

To present the data in a comparable way, Table 2.1 gives an overview of material intensities normalised per kW of turbine capacity. Out of the materials represented in the list, apart from oil (BMWi 2010; Tietenberg 2006) only magnetic materials appear to be critical (Jacobson and Delucchi 2011). Since there is already a broad range of literature on the oil market, peak oil and related scarcities (see for example Chapter 3 in OECD and IEA (2010b)), the focus of this work is on magnetic materials.

Although not all references listed in Table 2.1 provide information about magnetic materials, Jacobson and Delucchi (2011) mention that roughly 0.2 kg of neodymium are used per kW of a wind turbine's capacity.[2] Kleijn and Voet (2010) give a number of similar magnitude. When considering additional sources that do not provide a complete register of materials and are therefore not included in the table, it seems that data on the amount of rare earths in wind turbines vary, ranging from 0.2 to 3.3 kg of neodymium content per kW of rated capacity (Goonan 2011; Walters and Lusty 2010). All in all, publicly available

---

[1]Please note that the original data given in Schleisner (2000) apply to the wind farms as a whole and therefore have to be divided by the respective number of 500 kW turbines, i.e. 18 for the onshore and 10 for the offshore farm, in order to obtain data for a single power plant and derive material requirements per kW, as indicated in the table.

[2]They actually relate this amount to kWh instead of kW, which does not make sense from a technical point of view. Moreover, on the website they refer to, the unit is also kg/kW (Hatch 2009).

Material	Jacobson and Delucchi (2011)	Ardente et al. (2008)	Martínez et al. (2009)	Schleisner (2000)		Kleijn and Voet (2010)		Weinzettel et al. (2009)
				onshore	offshore	onshore	offshore	offshore
Steel	×	100.6	89.9	105.4	113.2	135.0	148.0	311.0
Concrete	×		350.0	565.0	1,130.0	306.0	1050.0	
Magnetic materials	0.2						0.15	
Aluminium	×	0.1		2.8	2.8	0.26	0.42	0.5
Copper	×	1.4	1.8	0.7	5.9	1.83	2.75	11.7
Wood epoxy, resin	×		6.6					0.3
Glass fiber	×	7.5	4.4					10.4
Plastic	×	0.1		4.0	4.0	1.92	2.09	1.8
Polyethylene					1.1			2.9
Iron		9.1	28.8	24.0	48.0			13.8
Oil products		0.2		0.2	0.2			15.0
Lead					6.7	0.0	3.79	2.6
Sand, gravel			0.2	4.2	4.2	0.0	150.0	646.0
Glass, ceramics				2.2	2.2			0.01
Logs (wood)								0.07
Others		0.6		1.4	1.4			0.05

Table 2.1: Material intensities for wind turbines. All numbers are given in kg/kW.

information on these data is quite sparse, so the estimates given have to be sufficient for the compilation of scenarios following in Chapter 4.

A review of other studies confirms the critical role magnetic materials play for wind turbines. For example, the USDE (2010) identifies praseodymium, neodymium, samarium and dysprosium to be employed in permanent magnets of wind power plants, but at the same time to come with availability restrictions. The report on "Critical raw materials for the EU" also concludes that rare earths, which the four previously mentioned materials belong to, are part of the most vulnerable group of natural resources for the EU (EC 2010).

Altogether, permanent magnets turn out to be the most critical part of a wind turbine. Since they are used for building the generator (Goonan 2011), the following section takes a closer look at this component.

2.2 Main generator types

This section provides a short overview of the technological background, but is restricted to the relevant aspects for understanding the economics in the subsequent chapters.

Figure 2.1 shows the constructive composition of a wind turbine. The component to concentrate on is the generator, situated in the back of the turbine. Its purpose is to convert mechanical energy, derived from the rotation of the blades, to electrical power (Herbert et al. 2007).

There are different types of generators used in wind power plants. Figure 2.2 shows the dimensions among which they can be distinguished.[3] First, the analysis is restricted to grid-connected wind power plants, i.e. those feeding power into the grid. A possible alternative are small-scale turbines for self-provision with electricity on the end user level. Those latter applications are not considered here. In the next step, the distinction is made according to the way the turbine is driven. This is generally possible via aerodynamic drag or aerodynamic lift. However, today's wind power plants work with the aerodynamic lift technology as the drag principle yields a much lower efficiency (Ackermann and Söder 2002; Hennicke et al. 2010).

On the subsequent level, wind turbines are distinguished into horizontal-axis and vertical-axis types. This classification refers to the position of the spin axis (WWEA 2006). Due to several disadvantages of vertical-axis turbines, they were only produced until the end of the 1980s and afterwards mostly replaced by horizontal-axis wind power plants (Ackermann

---

[3]For a more detailed technical explanation of the figure, see for example Ackermann and Söder (2002) and Bade et al. (2010).

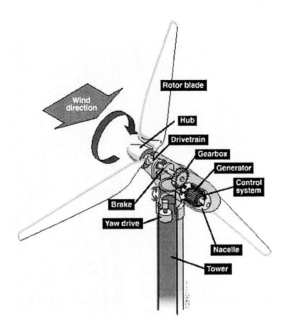

Figure 2.1: Parts of a wind turbine. Source: Ancona and McVeigh (2001).

and Söder 2002). The schematic wind turbine in Figure 2.1 belongs to the aerodynamic lift, horizontal axis type that is most common today.

Power control determines what kind of generator can be applied. It is necessary because wind turbines are designed to work most efficiently at a certain wind speed or range of wind speeds and have to be limited if the wind blows faster, so efficiency losses or, at even higher wind speeds, material damages can be avoided. The first option for power control is stall regulation, implying that the rotor blades are shaped such that at high wind speeds, turbulence causes the rotor to turn slower than it would otherwise do. Stall regulation requires constant rotational speed independent of the actual wind speed and therefore can only be used together with an asynchronous generator. The second possibility for power control is pitch regulation, allowing the blades to turn around their longitudinal axis and influencing the power output by moving into or out of the wind. A third concept combines stall and pitch regulation and is called active stall regulation. In this case, the blades can be pitched, which is useful at low wind speeds to increase energy yield, whereas at high wind speeds they are pitched into the opposite direction where the stall effect, produced by the special shape used in stall concepts, decelerates the rotor (Ackermann and Söder 2002). Active

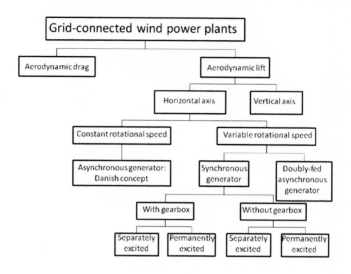

Figure 2.2: Categorisation of wind power plants. Source: compiled by the author, according to Ackermann and Söder (2002) and Bade et al. (2010).

stall control is primarily used for wind turbines in the megawatt classes and allows for a more accurate power regulation than pitch control (WWEA 2006). The pitch and active stall principles are usually combined with variable-speed generators, i.e. synchronous or doubly-fed asynchronous generators[4] (Leão et al. 2007). In general, grid-connected wind power plants are operated with either synchronous or asynchronous generators - out of which the doubly-fed asynchronous generator is only a special case - because these are the most robust and reliable types (Heier 2009).

Historically, stall regulated wind turbines with a directly grid-connected asynchronous generator were the first modern types, called "Danish concept" (Bade et al. 2010). They dominated the market until the mid-1990s (WWEA 2006). Main advantages were their simple design and robustness, guaranteeing operational reliability and low cost in serial production (Heier 2009). However, the optimal efficiency factor of a Danish concept turbine could only be obtained at a certain wind speed. To overcome this problem, some power plants were built with two generators that were constructed for different wind speeds to increase energy yield: depending on the actual wind speed, the generator that achieved the highest energy yield was turned on (Ackermann and Söder 2002; BWE 2011). That

---

[4]There is a third option to use an asynchronous generator with dynamic slip control, but this concept is rarely applied in practice and therefore neglected by the majority of the literature.

way, a capacity utilisation of about 35% could be achieved at maximum (NYSERDA 2005). A further drawback of the Danish concept was its sensitivity to storms or gusts; especially the blades and drive train were strained in strong winds. Moreover, the use of asynchronous generators and direct feed-in cause idle power, i.e. efficiency losses, and are not consistent any more with current grid standards in Europe (BWE 2011). Finally, the Danish concept is not applicable to wind turbines on the multi-megawatt scale (Ackermann and Söder 2002). Therefore, it has now been replaced by technologies with variable rotational speed.

The first generators to work with variable rotational speed, available from 1993 on, were synchronous. Only this kind of generator makes the gearbox[5] optional, i.e. enables so-called direct-drive wind turbines. The best known manufacturer in this segment is Enercon. Although synchronous generators are significantly more complex than traditional asynchronous ones (Heier 2009)[6] and are therefore more expensive (Ackermann and Söder 2002), they have considerable advantages: due to the variable rotational speed, the maximum energy yield is no longer restricted to one or two certain wind speeds, but can be maintained over a broad range of wind speeds (Ackermann and Söder 2002). Besides, synchronous generators are more efficient and have no problems with grid compatibility (WWEA 2006). They are also silent and robust because of few moving parts, and cooling is not necessary. Almost all synchronous generators used in wind power plants are ring generators and benefit from the omission of a gearbox (BWE 2011). As statistically most technical failures of wind turbines in Denmark and Germany are caused by gearbox problems, this is a major advantage (Herbert et al. 2007; Neumann et al. 2002).

Synchronous generators create a magnetic field that can either be separately or permanently excited. Separate excitation uses an electromagnet, predominantly made of copper, whereas permanent excitation requires permanent magnets (BWE 2011; Bade et al. 2010; Enercon 2010; WWEA 2006). Permanent magnets employed today mostly consist of neodymium, iron, and boron (Nd-Fe-B magnets, according to their symbols in the periodic table) (USDE 2010). Wind turbine manufacturers face a trade-off when deciding for either separate or permanent excitation: permanently excited generators, on the one hand, save about 25% weight, require no external power source and have a very high efficiency of 96-98%;[7] on the other hand, it is not possible to influence voltage via an external current (as there is none) and the materials, especially neodymium, are very expensive. For separately excited generators, the opposite is true (Bade et al. 2010; Hau 2008; Heier

---

[5]The gearbox turns the slow rotor movement into a faster movement the generator can deal with via gears of different sizes (Jacobson and Delucchi 2011).

[6]For example, in contrast to an asynchronous generator, a synchronous one needs a converter and complicated control systems (BWE 2011; WWEA 2006).

[7]As opposed to a maximum efficiency degree of 94% for separately excited synchronous generators, 95.5-96.5% for asynchronous generators, and 94-95.5% for doubly-fed asynchronous generators (Hau 2008). Note that those data apply to the efficiency of the generator alone and must not be confused with overall wind turbine capacity factors, as described below.

2009).

In 1996, a third concept arose, namely the doubly-fed asynchronous generator that also works with variable rotational speed. As a gearbox is essential for this type of wind turbine, the generator can be smaller and lighter than a synchronous one (BWE 2011; Bade et al. 2010). Again, like its traditional asynchronous counterpart, the doubly-fed asynchronous generator is simple and robust. Synchronisation with the grid frequency is only necessary for about 20-40% of nominal capacity, so the converter can also be smaller.[8] All in all, a doubly-fed asynchronous generator is available at low cost and is therefore used most often today, particularly in high power wind turbines (BWE 2011; WWEA 2006).

With respect to overall wind turbine efficiency as a function of generator type, the capacity factor is the measure to refer to. It states what fraction of its rated capacity a power plant will actually deliver during one year and depends on the particular characteristics of its location (EWEA 2009). For the aerodynamic lift concept, the theoretical upper limit that can be achieved in the case of an idealised turbine underlying no losses is defined by the Lanchester-Betz limit. According to this figure, the maximum power output accounts for $\frac{16}{27} = 59.3\%$ of rated capacity (Hennicke et al. 2010; Musgrove 2010; Wiser et al. 2011).

Figure 2.3 illustrates the capacity factor gains of wind turbines driven by permanent magnet generators relative to a doubly-fed asynchronous model. Kurronen et al. (2010) compare a doubly-fed induction generator (DFIG), a high-speed permanent magnet generator (PMG-HS), a medium-speed permanent magnet generator (PMG-MS), and a low-speed, direct-drive permanent magnet generator (PMG-DD). The authors assess their relative performance at locations with different wind speeds and highlight the optimal generator type for each site. As the figure shows, permanent magnet generators are superior at all sites, but yield advantages especially at low wind speeds.

Regarding costs, Heier (2009) states that cost per kilowatt generally decreases with increasing capacity, both for synchronous and asynchronous machines. However, cost differences between the two generator types emerge when considering a certain fixed capacity: for low capacities in the range of a few kilowatt, asynchronous machines have a clear advantage due to their simple design and serial production, but for higher capacities, both concepts reveal similar cost structures. One has to be careful, though, when interpreting these results because Heier (2009) neither declares if he refers to the traditional asynchronous generator or includes the doubly-fed asynchronous generator in his analysis, nor does he specify if he accounts for separately or permanently excited synchronous generators. As mentioned earlier, there are substantial differences in the cost structures depending on those dimensions. More specific data for different kinds of wind turbines are not available owing to non-disclosure on the part of manufacturers. There is merely an extensive model that has been created by Fingersh et al. (2006), providing formulae for

---

[8]A synchronous generator requires synchronisation of total nominal capacity.

2 MW Drive Train with Different Generator Types	DFIG	PMG-HS	PMG-MS	PMG-DD
	Average Wind Speed 5.4 m/s			
Annual Energy Production	2435 MWh	2549 MWh	2636 MWh	2641 MWh
Comparison with DFIG	100.0%	104.7%	108.3%	108.5%
	Average Wind Speed 6.8 m/s			
Annual Energy Production	4041 MWh	4146 MWh	4263 MWh	4233 MWh
Comparison with DFIG	100.0%	102.6%	105.2%	104.3%
	Average Wind Speed 8.2 m/s			
Annual Energy Production	5338 MWh	5427 MWh	5566 MWh	5499 MWh
Comparison with DFIG	100.0%	101.7%	104.3%	103.0%

Figure 2.3: Capacity factor gains of wind turbines driven by permanent magnet generators relative to doubly-fed asynchronous models. Source: Kurronen et al. (2010). The abbreviations stand for the different generator types: DFIG - doubly-fed induction generator, PMG - permanent magnet generator, HS - high speed, MS - medium speed, DD - direct drive.

the cost calculation of wind turbine components for different generator types, depending on machine rating and rotor diameter.

The incidence of rare earth elements in wind power plants, i.e. the importance of permanently excited synchronous generators, will be covered after accounting for differences between onshore and offshore wind turbines as they also determine material requirements.

2.3 Particularities of offshore turbines

Whereas onshore wind power refers to turbines situated on land, offshore is defined as wind power at the sea. Some authors distinguish between actual offshore - where the wind power plants have to stand at least 30 km from the coast - and so-called nearshore applications closer to the coast (Heier 2009; Neumann et al. 2002). As onshore potentials for wind power in Europe are largely exploited already, offshore wind power can contribute to continued growth of the market (Bilgili et al. 2011; Ender 2011; Tryfonidou and Wagner n.d.). This is particularly important from the perspective of climate change mitigation, where the further expansion of wind power plays an important role (Wiser et al. 2011).

Moving from onshore to offshore applications yields several advantages. To name only the most important aspects, wind speeds at the sea are usually higher than on land, there is less turbulence and huge areas are available, so the overall potential of electricity production is higher than onshore. Furthermore, there are no problems associated with resistance by residents or real estate owners (Ackermann and Söder 2002; Bade et al. 2010; Bilgili et al. 2011; WWEA 2006).

Nevertheless, the offshore environment poses certain challenges to the construction of wind turbines due to waves, tide, ice, a varying water line, soil properties, air humidity and salinity, stronger winds and restricted accessibility. An additional challenge arises especially for Germany because in contrast to other European coastal regions, water depths increase very quickly with increasing distance from the shore, making the positioning of wind power plants even more difficult. Another aspect to consider is grid integration; a solution has to be found for transporting the electricity to the coast with a minimum of efficiency losses and maintenance effort (Bade et al. 2010; Bilgili et al. 2011; Heier 2009; Neumann et al. 2002; Rehfeldt et al. 2001).

All those conditions have to be accounted for when designing an offshore turbine. In general, there are two possible ways to construct an offshore wind power plant: manufacturers can either rely on robust, well-proven onshore turbines and adjust them for marine requirements (an example is REpower 5M), or they can design new concepts specifically for offshore purposes (e.g. Multibrid M5000). In practice, the first way is the most frequent procedure (Bade et al. 2010). In both cases, however, technological features of offshore power plants differ only slightly from those of onshore turbines. The most important modifications concern a solid supporting structure, i.e. tower and foundation,[9] and protection of electric components from moisture (Ackermann and Söder 2002; Bade et al. 2010; Bilgili et al. 2011; Neumann et al. 2002). A direct comparison of an onshore and offshore turbine's material requirements can be found in Schleisner (2000) and Kleijn and Voet (2010) (see summary in Table 2.1). It shows that an offshore wind power plant differs from an onshore turbine of the same capacity predominantly in the use of bulk materials like concrete, gravel, iron and lead, but also copper, thereby indicating the importance of tower and foundation adjustment to a larger scale. The high amount of copper may be due to long submarine cables. These offshore modifications do not affect critical material requirements as onshore and offshore turbines use the same generator types and will continue to do so in the near term (Angerer et al. 2009). However, the use of low-maintenance components is particularly important for offshore applications as at some sites accessibility is limited to 120 days per year (Neumann et al. 2002). Therefore, gearless generator concepts

---

[9]An overview of special tower concepts can be found in Arvizu et al. (2011) and Neumann et al. (2002). Future development is widely expected to make greater water depths accessible, which could be implemented via floating platforms that are not fixed at the sea floor with a monopile construction, as is most common today, but rather behave like a buoy (Bilgili et al. 2011; Weinzettel et al. 2009; Wiser et al. 2011).

with permanent magnets are especially attractive because of their robustness and high efficiency (cf. the use of permanent magnet materials assumed exclusively for offshore wind
power by Kleijn and Voet (2010)). It can be estimated that with the continuous development of offshore wind power those generator concepts become increasingly widespread
(Akhmatov et al. 2003; Leão et al. 2007). Out of the eight offshore turbine types currently
employed, two already rely on permanently excited synchronous generators and one model
is gearless (Dena 2011).

With respect to the economics of wind power, the main offshore-specific cost drivers include:

- foundations

- grid integration, i.e. transformer stations and sea transmission cables

- installation and maintenance efforts

Since with growing distance from the shore water depths increase and weather conditions
become more and more rough, costs rise as well. However, they are always site-specific
due to the particularities of certain coastal areas. To name a German example, in the North
Sea waves are usually higher than in the Baltic Sea, but floating ice is more common in
the Baltic Sea. On the other hand, placing wind power plants at locations further from the
shore also yields advantages because wind speeds increase (Bilgili et al. 2011; Eerens and
Uslu 2009; Neumann et al. 2002).

In general, costs of offshore wind power plants are estimated to account for 150 to 300%
of onshore costs (Bilgili et al. 2011; EWEA 2009; Eerens and Uslu 2009; Wiser et al.
2011). Yet, efficiency is also higher, partly compensating for the additional cost: whereas
the capacity factor of a typical onshore turbine is approximately 25%, it is in the range of
30 to 40% for offshore applications (Bade et al. 2010; Weinzettel et al. 2009). The most
adequate measure for a comparison of onshore and offshore costs is the levelised cost of
electricity (LCOE), expressed in monetary units per unit of energy (Wiser et al. 2011). It
takes the following factors into consideration (Arvizu et al. 2011; EWEA 2009):

- annual energy production

- investment costs

- operation and maintenance costs

- financing costs

- economic lifetime of the power plant

- discount rate

The LCOE incorporates "all private costs that accrue upstream in the value chain of electricity production" except for transmission and distribution costs (Bruckner et al. 2011).[10] Table 2.2 lists the individual LCOE components and the resulting overall costs for onshore and offshore wind power as given by Bruckner et al. (2011). Their range of results is confirmed by REN21 (2010) who calculate typical onshore costs between \$0.05/kWh and \$0.09/kWh; offshore cost estimates are between \$0.10/kWh and \$0.14/kWh.

	Onshore	Offshore
Capacity factor (%)[a]	20-40	35-45
Investment cost ($\$_{2005}$/kW)	1,200-2,100	3,200-5,000
Operation and maintenance cost ($\$_{2005}$/kWh)	0.012-0.023	0.020-0.040
Power plant lifetime (years)	20	20
Discount rate (%)	3-10	3-10
LCOE ($\$_{2005}$/kWh)	0.05-0.15	0.10-0.20

Table 2.2: LCOE of onshore and offshore wind power plants. Source: Bruckner et al. (2011).

[a] As a measure of energy production.

At good sites, onshore wind power is already competitive with fossil power generation even if external costs are not taken into consideration. Offshore wind power is still lagging behind and requires further innovation to become competitive (Arvizu et al. 2011; Bade et al. 2010).

As offshore costs exceed those of onshore power plants significantly, economic operation requires sufficiently large turbines to achieve economies of scale (Wiser et al. 2011) in terms of higher yields that compensate for the additional costs (Heier 2009; Neumann et al. 2002; Tryfonidou and Wagner n.d.).[11] Leão et al. (2007) specify that offshore turbines should have a capacity of at least 3 MW to ensure efficiency; Bade et al. (2010) even mention 5 MW turbines as the minimum for cost-effective operation because of a high share of fixed costs.

---

[10] Although output subsidies and tax exemptions are eliminated from LCOE calculations, it is still possible that indirect benefits to the inputs of electricity generation cannot be completely excluded (Bruckner et al. 2011).

[11] Large-scale offshore applications are justified because larger construction types of wind turbines usually coincide with higher rated power (Hennicke et al. 2010).

2.4 Recapitulation

Rare earths have been identified as the most vulnerable input material for wind turbines. They are employed in the generator. Nowadays, two different concepts are applied: doubly-fed asynchronous and synchronous generators. The latter can further be subdivided according to their use of electromagnets or permanent magnets. Only permanently excited synchronous generators require rare earths. Their major advantages are high efficiency and robustness. However, production of wind power plants driven by a permanent-magnet generator is more expensive, thus inducing a trade-off from the perspective of manufacturers and clients.

With the increasing deployment of offshore wind turbines and their associated particularities like restricted access, it can be expected that permanently excited generators as a low-maintenance component will be used more frequently in the future. Although gearless designs on both onshore and offshore markets totalled only about 10% of turbines produced in 2009, it is already perceptible that they are becoming increasingly popular (REN21 2010). Out of the ten global market leaders in wind turbine manufacturing, the majority already employs permanent magnet generators or is investigating the technology (Kurronen et al. 2010).

3 Market analysis of rare earth elements

Having provided the main technical foundations of wind turbines in Chapter 2, we subsequently proceed to analysing the particularities of the market for rare earth elements (REEs) since they are among the most vulnerable materials.

First of all, the term "rare earth elements" has to be clarified. It is actually a misleading name (Angerer et al. 2009) because the elements belonging to this group are quite abundant in the earth's crust; however, they generally occur in such small concentrations that most deposits are not worth mining solely for their REE content (Cordier 2011a,b; Haxel et al. 2002). Within ore deposits, REEs tend to occur as compounds (Liedtke and Elsner 2009).

The REE group consists of 17 chemical elements that are characterised by similar properties (Walters and Lusty 2010). It comprises the 15 lanthanides as well as scandium and yttrium. Table 3.1 gives an overview of the single elements together with their atomic number and symbol in the periodic table of the elements (Cordier 2011a; Liedtke and Elsner 2009). Due to the REEs' conjoint occurrence and similar properties, the extraction of one special element is very difficult and capital-intensive (Liedtke and Elsner 2009; London 2010; Walters and Lusty 2010).

Depending on the respective element, the crustal abundance of REEs ranges from 0.5 ppm to 60 ppm. Neodymium as the most important REE for permanent magnets has an abundance of 28 ppm. Copper, by comparison, is ranked at 50 ppm (Cordier 2011a). As these data illustrate, the occurrence of single REEs may vary widely. A rough classification can be made corresponding to the atomic numbers: as a rule of thumb, REEs with even atomic numbers are more abundant than those with odd atomic numbers (Haxel et al. 2002; Walters and Lusty 2010).

Moreover, light and heavy REEs can be distinguished, the former containing atomic numbers 57 to 64 and the latter comprising atomic numbers 65 to 71 plus yttrium (Cordier 2011a; Walters and Lusty 2010).[1] Concerning these groups, it can be stated that the concentration of light REEs is usually higher than that of heavy REEs (Haxel et al. 2002; Liedtke and Elsner 2009; Walters and Lusty 2010). Accordingly, the majority of REE deposits has an 80 to 99% content of just four elements, namely lanthanum, cerium, praseodymium and neodymium (Haxel et al. 2002).

---

[1] Scandium is not included in this kind of classification (Cordier 2011a).

Name of element	Atomic number and symbol	Name of element	Atomic number and symbol
lanthanum	$_{57}$La	dysprosium	$_{66}$Dy
cerium	$_{58}$Ce	holmium	$_{67}$Ho
praseodymium	$_{59}$Pr	erbium	$_{68}$Er
neodymium	$_{60}$Nd	thulium	$_{69}$Tm
promethium[a]	$_{61}$Pm	ytterbium	$_{70}$Yb
samarium	$_{62}$Sm	lutetium	$_{71}$Lu
europium	$_{63}$Eu	scandium	$_{21}$Sc
gadolinium	$_{64}$Gd	yttrium	$_{39}$Y
terbium	$_{65}$Tb		

Table 3.1: List of rare earth elements. Source: compiled by the author, according to data from Cordier (2011a) and Liedtke and Elsner (2009).

[a]Unstable element.

REEs can either be produced as rare earth oxides (REOs) or as rare earth metals (REMs). REMs can further be subdivided into individual products, i.e. a pure metal consisting of only one element, and metal compounds that are called *mischmetal* (Angerer et al. 2009) whereby mischmetal is a mixture of different REEs as it naturally occurs (Papp et al. 2008). The only REEs produced as individual metals are lanthanum, cerium, neodymium and yttrium. Together they comprise about a quarter of total production (Angerer et al. 2009).

In the following, a comprehensive market overview is presented to account for the special forces on the REE market. From the confrontation of supply- and demand-side influences, consequences for the price path are deduced. As it turns out that the REE market is characterised by substantial imbalances, mitigation options to combat this problem are evaluated.[2] Finally, an outlook on the future market development is given, leading over to Chapter 4 where different options for the future wind turbine deployment are assessed.

3.1 The supply side

Since raw materials are unequally distributed across the earth, their supply is commonly subject to vulnerability. There are many potential disturbances: global companies may arise trying to obtain market power, suppliers may delay deliveries, or producing countries

---

[2]In contrast to its meaning in climate policy analyses conducted with economic models such as ReMIND-R, mitigation in this context does not stand for an emission reduction target. The term is rather used in a broader sense to describe possibilities for easing the problems that arise from the market imbalance.

may be politically unstable, to name just a few examples. Additionally, due to the market's global interconnections, policy measures taken by single governments can hardly exert influence. This framework poses particularly big problems in the case of resources with limited substitutability (Angerer et al. 2009).

The market for REEs is highly vulnerable in this respect because currently 97% of mine production originate from one country - China (Liedtke and Elsner 2009). This fact results in a notable import dependency for most other countries. Predominantly industrialised countries with a substantial share of high tech industries are affected, e.g. the USA as well as many EU member states are 100% import-reliant (Angerer et al. 2009; Cordier 2011b; EC 2008).

As the previously mentioned criticality of REEs is mainly caused by supply-side problems (Behrendt et al. 2007), the market analysis starts with this issue.

3.1.1 Reserves and resources

For an assessment of available quantities of a certain material in the earth's crust, the measures of reserves and resources are central. Figure 3.1 illustrates how the dimensions are interrelated. Reserves indicate the geologically registered amount of a material that can be exploited both technically and economically under currently prevailing conditions (Behrendt et al. 2007; EC 2010). The resulting number will therefore vary over time, depending on technology and price levels, so it must not be misinterpreted as an indicator of absolute scarcity (Moriarty and Honnery 2011). Resources, on the other hand, encompass reserves plus additional identified deposits where mining might become possible in the future, provided that technological progress and rising prices ensure economic efficiency (Behrendt et al. 2007; EC 2010). As Rogner (1997) points out, there is a positive feedback effect between prices, reserves and resources: as raw material prices rise, the extraction of previously unprofitable resources becomes cost-effective, reclassifying them as reserves, while at the same time the incentive to pursue exploration activities is enhanced, thereby facilitating technological progress. Theoretically, under the assumption of an infinitely high price, the total resource could be exhausted (Tietenberg 2006). On an intermediate level between reserves and resources, the reserve base, comprising reserves, is the share of resources complying with minimum standards to be exploited today or in the near future (Behrendt et al. 2007; EC 2010). Finally, on the uppermost level, the resource base adds to the resources the amount of undiscovered resources, i.e. it measures the overall abundance of a material in the earth's crust (EC 2010) and is therefore a geological rather than an economically determined dimension (Tietenberg 2006). Just like reserves, resources are a time-dependent measure since formerly unknown deposits can be discovered (EC 2010), augmenting the resource stock and diminishing the stock of undiscovered resources accordingly.[3] It is also evident that there are no data for the resource base as no one can determine with certainty the amount of undiscovered resources.

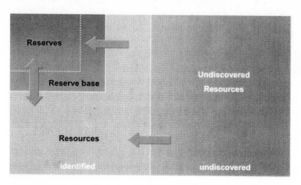

Figure 3.1: Relation of reserves, reserve base, resources, and resource base. Source: EC (2010).

Another frequently-cited measure is the reserves-to-production ratio, stating for how many years today's reserves will suffice to maintain the current level of demand (Behrendt et al. 2007). Yet, this is not a reliable figure because it neglects any technological progress, including new recycling and substitution possibilities, as well as changes in the price level that may occur over time (Behrendt et al. 2007; Wacker and Blank 1999). The resources-to-production ratio is defined analagously (Angerer et al. 2009).

Applying these measures to REEs, one has to bear in mind that they are a depletable resource, which means that natural replenishment can be disregarded within a time horizon relevant for humans. Dynamic efficiency therefore requires the maximisation of the present value of net benefits gained from REEs, implying a balance of today's and tomorrow's uses (Tietenberg 2006). As a foundation for the allocative decision, Table 3.2 summarises the values of the defined categories for REEs.[4] Data for single elements are unfortunately not available (Angerer et al. 2009). It has to be noted that statistical data are usually provided in REO equivalents, whereby the REE-to-REO ratio is about 1:0.85, but both terms are usually treated as approximate equivalents (Goonan 2011).

---

[3] As a recent example has proven, even the discovery of one single deposit can have a major influence on the data (EC 2010): in 2011, additional REE sources of significant scale have been found on the ground of the Pacific Ocean, near Hawaii and Tahiti. In a depth of 3,500 to 6,000 m, about 100 billion t have been identified. The area covers 11 million km^2 and it is estimated that due to the high REE concentration 1 km^2 could satisfy 20% of current worldwide demand. However, it has not been explored yet whether mining the deposit is technically feasible (Tagesschau 2011b).

[4] It should be noted that the aforementioned discovery of new REE deposits in the Pacific Ocean does not affect reserves data as their exploitability is not given yet. However, the amount of resources has increased, so the resources-to-production ratio is meanwhile probably higher than stated here.

Measure	Value	Unit
Reserves	88,000,000	t REO
Reserve base	150,000,000	t REO
Reserves-to-production ratio	715	yr
Resources-to-production ratio	1,220	yr

Table 3.2: Reserve and resource data for REEs. Source: compiled by the author, according to data from Angerer et al. (2009), Behrendt et al. (2007) and Kurronen et al. (2010).

In the context of this thesis it is also relevant to identify the geographical distribution of reserves. Table 3.3 presents the most recent available data. Although almost half of the total reserves is currently concentrated in China, the remaining deposits are widely dispersed (Walters and Lusty 2010). To account for the regional concentration of reserves, the Herfindahl-Hirschman Index (HHI) is a commonly used benchmark. It is calculated as the sum of the squared shares of raw materials occurrence within the corresponding countries, but can as well be applied to raw materials production or market power of companies (Rosenau-Tornow et al. 2009). As the respective shares are written as fractions, the HHI can cover a range between 0 and 1 with a larger value indicating a smaller number of agents with correspondingly more market power each (Tour et al. 2011). For the concentration of REO reserves, Angerer et al. (2009) report a HHI of 0.23, i.e. a moderate value.

Although the reserve distribution gives useful insight into the mining potential, actual mine production figures are more significant for evaluating the current situation on the market. There is a wide consensus in literature that reserve- and resource-related scarcities will not play a major role in the foreseeable future, but possible shortages may rather arise from production bottlenecks (see e.g. Behrendt et al. (2007), EC (2008), and Tietenberg (2006)). Table 3.4 illustrates the amount of REOs extracted by country. Owing to non-disclosure of data by some countries, the table has to remain incomplete.[5] Furthermore, figures are often estimated and may differ depending on the source; in case of inconsistent data, the most recent figures were selected or, if there were several sources dating from the same year, the one that seemed to harmonise best with pre-existing data was chosen.

As Table 3.4 indicates, China plays the role of a quasi-monopolist on the REE market, accounting for more than 95% of supply in any of the six recent years. The implications of this phenomenon are discussed in detail in Section 3.1.2.

When considering a rather long-run perspective, between 1990 and 2006 global REO mining expanded on average by 7% annually (Goonan 2011); from 1992 to 2008 total world

---

[5]Data for CIS and the category "Others" were not available at all.

Country	Reserves (t REO)
China	55,000,000
CIS[a]	19,000,000
USA	13,000,000
India	3,100,000
Australia	1,600,000
Brazil	48,000
Malaysia	30,000
Others	22,000,000
Total[b]	113,778,000

Table 3.3: Geographical distribution of REE reserves. Source: compiled by the author, according to data from Cordier (2011b).

[a]Commonwealth of Independent States.

[b]Total figure has been calculated by the author and does not comply with the reserve data from Table 3.2 since the latter mainly relies on data from 2009 and 2010. However, as more recent data for reserve base, reserves-to-production ratio and resources-to-production ratio were not available, the older reserve figure has been kept in the previous table to assure consistency within Table 3.2.

production increased by more than 100% with the maximum being reached in 2006 (Walters and Lusty 2010). To give an impression of the importance of single REEs, Figure 3.2 shows their share of total REE production in 2010.[6]

As mentioned previously, REEs usually occur as compounds, which means that the extraction of one particular element is not only determined by its own economics, but also by those of its co-products. Secondly, REE compounds are itself by-products of other minerals (EC 2010), so the same interdependence applies on a higher level as well. Thirdly, it has already been shown that China possesses significant market power, and fourthly, the extraction and processing of REEs causes external effects, most notably environmental damage (Lohse 2011b). Hence, there are four particularities to consider on the REE market. The subsequent section takes a closer look at market failure arising from these circumstances.

---

[6]The data illustrated here do not contradict the statement in the introductory section of Chapter 3 that lanthanum, cerium, neodymium and yttrium as individual metals together comprise a quarter of total production; they are additionally produced as REOs or within mischmetal, and Figure 3.2 accounts for overall production.

Country	2005	2006	2007	2008	2009	2010
China	119,000	133,000	120,000	125,000	129,000	130,000
	97.5%	97.1%	96.8%	97.6%	95.6%	97.0%
India	2,700	2,700	2,700	2,700	2,700	2,700
	2.2%	1.9%	2.2%	2.1%	2.0%	2.0%
Russia	n.a.	n.a.	n.a.	n.a.	2,470	n.a.
					1.8%	
Brazil	527	527	645	550	550	550
	0.4%	0.4%	0.5%	0.4%	0.4%	0.4%
Malaysia	150	430	380	233	350	350
	0.1%	0.3%	0.3%	0.2%	0.3%	0.3%
Total	122,000	137,000	124,000	128,000	135,000	134,000

Table 3.4: Mine production by country. Source: compiled by the author, according to data from Cordier (2011a), Cordier (2011b), USDE (2010) and Walters and Lusty (2010). For each country the first row indicates the absolute amount in t REO, the second row refers to the country's share of the known world production in the respective year. Since data for Russia are only available for 2009, affecting total world production and the countries' shares only in that year, intertemporal comparability is limited. Due to rounding the shares may not add up to 100%.

3.1.2 Mining, processing, international trade, and market failure

Co-production. Current production levels are not sufficient to cope with increasing demand for several REEs. Above all, neodymium, dysprosium, europium and terbium are facing excess demand (Cordier 2011a).[7] Whereas production increased by a factor of 2.45 between 1990 and 2000, demand for neodymium and dysprosium as magnet materials expanded by a factor of 9 to 10 in the same time period (Angerer et al. 2009) and has further accelerated since then (London 2010). Owing to their status as co-products, i.e. the fact that multiple individual REEs occur as a bundle (USDE 2010; Walters and Lusty 2010), the price of a certain REE depends on the prices of the elements it is combined with, the respective abundance of each material in the ore, and separation and refining costs of the whole package. If REEs are to be extracted, the main driver is often neodymium because of its use in a wide range of applications (USDE 2010). Yet co-production implies that according to the composition of the ore deposit, further REEs are "unintentionally" extracted, too. Thereby a situation of excess supply is provoked on the markets of the other, less desired elements, causing their prices to fall accordingly, which yields a feedback effect on the economics of the originally desired product. All in all, about 25% of REEs

---

[7]Demand-side patterns are examined in Section 3.2.

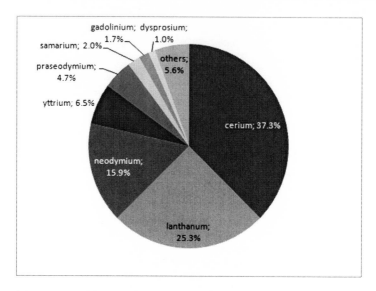

Figure 3.2: Estimated REE production by element in 2010. Source: compiled by the author, according to data from USDE (2010).

extracted are in excess supply (Angerer et al. 2009).

By-production. Similarly, the availability of by-products depends on the characteristics of the main product. By-products are typically characterised by a low price elasticity of supply because production is primarily targeted at the main product and thus reacts basically to incentives on the main product's market (EC 2008). However, the role of by-products must not be underestimated either: apart from the market conditions of the primary product, prices, ore grade and recovery rates of by-products also influence their extraction, though possibly to a moderate extent (Papp et al. 2008). By-products can, on the one hand, provide supplementary revenue for the producer, but on the other hand they induce higher production costs (EC 2010). REEs appear as by-products of four main minerals: bastnäsite, monazite, xenotime, and ion absorption clays (Angerer et al. 2009; USDE 2010). An isolated examination of individual REEs independent from their co- and by-products is therefore not possible.

Chinese quasi-monopoly. On the markets for raw materials, concentration both on country and company level is widely spread (EC 2008). Concerning global REO production from a historical perspective (see also Figure 3.3), a trend toward dominating exporters can already be observed from the mid-1960s on, when the Mountain Pass mine in California started operations. The USA quickly became the primary producer of REOs until in the mid-1980s China entered the world market, gradually crowding out competitors by means of its extraordinarily low production costs that were feasible due to low labour and energy costs as well as minor legal standards regarding environmental protection and mining permission (Aston 2010; Cordier 2011a; Haxel et al. 2002). Finally, since the beginning of the 1990s, China has been dominating the market to an increasing extent.

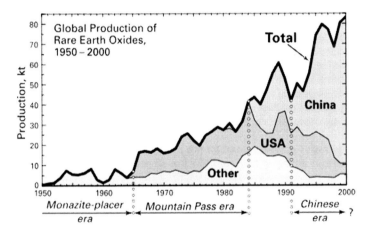

Figure 3.3: Historical development of global REO production. Source: Haxel et al. (2002).

Today, China has gained a market share of 97% (Liedtke and Elsner 2009) and profits from its abundant endowment with REE deposits, supporting the rapid deployment of electronics and other industries in Asia (Haxel et al. 2002). As domestic demand for raw materials is substantial because of the prevalent extension of infrastructure (Papp et al. 2008), China predominantly strives for self-sufficiency of raw materials to ensure that its development can be maintained independent of imports (London 2010). Besides, China engages in REE mining projects abroad and encourages processing of REEs within its own borders (Liedtke and Elsner 2009).

Whereas foreign investment in REE extraction is confined, it is facilitated in the value-added manufacturing sector processing REEs (USDE 2010). REE processing to the point of semi-fabrication is mainly carried out within China, whereas the production of assemblies is internationally distributed (Goonan 2011). However, manufacturing of sintered neodymium-iron-boron (Nd-Fe-B) magnets is subject to intellectual property rights and therefore exclusively conducted by ten licensed companies in China, Japan and Germany (USDE 2010). Domestic demand for permanent magnets in China has soared since 2008, while at the same time magnet exports dropped (Cordier 2011a). Moreover, China takes over an increasing share of wind turbine production: while in 2007 only 10% of the world's wind turbines came from China, the figure has steeply risen to 30% in 2009 (REN21 2010).

REE extraction in China is primarily undertaken in two mines, the largest share being covered by Bayan Obo in Inner Mongolia; this deposit contains the majority of Chinese REE reserves (EC 2010; Haxel et al. 2002) and yielded more than 40% of total world-wide production in 2007 (Liedtke and Elsner 2009). The second main deposit is located in the tropical southern part of China, predominantly in the provinces Longnan and Jiangxi where especially high concentrations of the less abundant heavy REEs occur, making it a valuable source (Haxel et al. 2002; Liedtke and Elsner 2009). Furthermore, in the south of China several smaller and partly illegal mines are operated, smuggling their output abroad (Milmo 2010; USDE 2010). In 2008 approximately one third of Chinese REE exports was smuggled (Walters and Lusty 2010). The government tries to subdue these activities and has already initiated the closure of illegal mines and the merger of mine-operating companies under state control (Hein 2010).

Owing to the high domestic demand for raw materials, China has imposed export restrictions and charges an export tariff on REEs that ranges between 15 and 25%, depending on the material under consideration (London 2010; USDE 2010). Additionally, import tariffs on 600 construction materials and components are levied (Tagesschau 2010b), thereby creating a competitive advantage for domestic intermediate products.

Another kind of export restriction arises from the export quotas assigned by the government. In the past, they have steadily been reduced (Milmo 2010) and are supposed to be cut by another 2 to 3% every year since China expressed plans to pay more attention to resource protection and establish a strategic domestic REE stockpile (Tagesschau 2010a; USDE 2010). Between 2003 and 2009, REE exports already dropped by 40%; whereas originally 75% of REE production were available for export, the fraction meanwhile has declined to about 25% (Milmo 2010), reaching 30,258 t REO in 2010 (USDE 2010).[8]

The various kinds of export restrictions have already brought the World Trade Organization (WTO) to the scene. The distortion of competition by China has sharply been criticised because both the higher raw materials prices on the world market and the impact of artificial shortages on downstream industries imply a subsidisation of Chinese companies that are of course not subject to the export constraints. This violates WTO directives as well as certain commitments China had to agree to upon its WTO accession (EC 2010). There

---

[8]The quota for 2011 is still under discussion.

are also initiatives on the part of individual governments to negotiate higher export quotas with the Chinese administration (Tagesschau 2011a).

From the perspective of importers, the security of supply of Chinese REEs depends on its political and economic stability and its willingness to cooperate with other countries (Haxel et al. 2002). The EC (2010) suggests to use the Worldbank Worldwide Governance Indicator as a reference point to judge these patterns. The most recent data for the category "political stability" are from 2010 and rank China 8th among the 10 largest economies in the world as defined by GDP. When considering all countries, China appears in the 10th to 25th percentile[9] in 2010, the worst rating since 1996 (The World Bank Group 2011a,b). A recent example for China's arbitrary behaviour on the raw materials markets can be seen in its relation to Japan: after China had already drastically cut RE metal shipments to Japan in 2008 (Cordier 2011a), political controversies between both countries in 2010 resulted in a complete blockade of RE minerals exports lasting three weeks (Aston 2010).

In addition to market power on the country level, a concentration is also observable at the company level, whereby the two aspects are closely interrelated. Chinese REE companies represent a market share of 97% (Liedtke and Elsner 2009) and are de facto treated like state corporations. Besides the negative implication of market control, this combination also results in financial solidity, which is essential for firms operating on the volatile REE market (EC 2010). The largest share of REE exports is covered by Inner Mongolia Baotou Steel Rare Earth International Trade Company, the central institution to coordinate purchase and marketing of REOs and metals from the Baotou region (Cordier 2011a). Several other national corporations exist in China, though their individual market power is rather limited with the exception of Ganzhou Rare Earths Co. (Liedtke and Elsner 2009). The remaining 3% of supply on the global REE market are shared among Indian state corporations with about 2%, a Brazilian firm with less than 1% and some small Western enterprises (Liedtke and Elsner 2009; London 2010).

In order to circumvent Chinese export quotas and reduce the import dependency of REE-processing industries, importing countries pursuit several strategies. One option is to invest in foreign mining projects, thereby securing raw materials supply; another possibility is the build-up of national inventories for critical resources (Behrendt et al. 2007). Furthermore, many binational long-term delivery contracts exist (EC 2008).[10] An ultimate alternative would be to move REE-dependent companies to China, so they are not subject to export restrictions any more, which is up to now only a theoretical consideration (Hein 2010; Walters and Lusty 2010). Additionally, REE importers strive for higher material efficiency along the whole product life cycle as well as the development of economic recycling technologies on a large scale (Angerer et al. 2009; EC 2008, 2010); selected mitigation potentials are analysed in more detail in Section 3.4.

---

[9]The higher the assigned percentile, the better political stability in a country is judged.

[10]For an overview of national strategies implemented in individual countries, see USDE (2010).

Negative externalities. On top of the market failure associated with the aforementioned particularities - co-production, by-production, and quasi-monopolistic market power - the REE industry is characterised by another drawback, namely external effects in the form of environmental burden. Resource exhaustion often raises a conflict with sustainability (Angerer et al. 2009), but as there are very few suppliers on the international REE market, thus having the chance to act strategically, the problem is reinforced: a global policy for sustainable mining and trading is hardly enforceable (Behrendt et al. 2007).

Environmental damage is caused by the REE sector along two stages of the supply chain, extraction and processing. Starting at the point of mining, radioactivity is released when REEs are extracted from monazite. Monazite contains thorium as a further by-product, which is only weakly radioactive itself, but occurs in compound with highly radioactive intermediate daughter products. Therefore monazite deposits have largely ceased to be exploited (Haxel et al. 2002).

Moreover, the extraction, separation and refinement of REEs require the use of chemicals that leave behind toxic sludge. The waste products often end up in the ground water, causing pollution of the environment, disease and poisoning of the local population, and contamination of farmland (Lohse 2011b; Walters and Lusty 2010).

Finally, REE production is very energy-intensive. However, the majority of energy in China originates from coal-fired power plants (Walters and Lusty 2010), so the whole process contributes to air pollution and the greenhouse effect.

Regarding the environmental performance of countries, there is a similar index like the Worldbank Worldwide Governance Indicator. The Yale Center for Environmental Law and Policy at Yale University regularly publishes the Environmental Performance Index (EC 2010). It provides a measure for the proximity of countries to environmental policy goals from the areas of environmental public health and ecosystem vitality. The most recent results date from 2010, ranking China 121st out of 163 countries, or in the 4th out of 5 groups. Since the previous assessment in 2008 it has even been downgraded, indicating a degradation of environmental performance over time (Yale University and Columbia University 2011). Yet, in March 2011 China released new environmental standards that have been in force since October 2011 and set emission limits for 15 pollutants, affecting 60% of Chinese REE-producing companies (Lohse 2011b).

It should also be noted that REEs not only harm the environment, but are increasingly used to enable energy-efficient and emission-reducing technologies (Walters and Lusty 2010).[11] Hence the overall effect has to be considered, although it is difficult to offset both aspects and calculate the net impact. To the knowledge of the author this has not been done yet. There are however consistent claims in the life cycle literature on wind turbines (that in some cases employ RE permanent magnets) confirming the superior role of wind

---

[11] See Section 3.2.2.

power among different electricity-producing technologies with regard to criteria such as environmental footprint, sustainability issues and external cost (Arvizu et al. 2011; EC 2003; Jacobson 2009; Weinzettel et al. 2009).[12]

When the consequences of raw materials extraction and processing are assessed in literature, the analysis is mostly restricted to the associated negative externalities and ignores the following supply chain integration, which may be justified by the fact that subsequent positive effects often do not benefit the same people whose utility has decreased due to negative external effects from production. There the question arises how to define the society whose welfare is to be maximised: in case the world population is considered as a whole, the net effect may either be positive or negative, but if the population of a mining region is regarded individually, the welfare effect might well be detrimental.

Based on the assumption that the true social cost of raw materials exceeds their market price, owing to environmental burden and unconditional dependency of certain industries, economic theory offers a solution for correcting market failure. Tietenberg (2006) proposes to impose an import tariff on the materials under consideration and use the revenue to finance a national stockpile. That way, on the one hand the importing country can ensure continuous supply,[13] on the other hand research efforts for substitutes and probably also domestic production of raw materials are facilitated. Eventually, this strategy also conforms to the polluter-pays principle as the tariff is borne by those who demand the critical materials or their derivatives.[14] Yet in practice it is difficult to calculate the optimum tariff rate since pollution is not the only externality on the REE market. The existence of market power can to a certain degree countervail environmental degradation (Tietenberg 2006) because due to the quasi-monopoly, REE production would be inefficiently low in the absence of further kinds of market failure, but the negative externality implies that the quantity resulting from perfect competition would be inefficiently high. Thus an import tariff has to be adjusted to the net effect.

---

[12]The methodology of those assessments is often not made transparent, so it cannot be guaranteed that all of the studies include raw materials extraction impacts and account for the fact that some wind turbines contain REEs and others do not. As mentioned previously, the detailed analysis of environmental impacts of REEs still constitutes a gap in literature.

[13]USDE (2010) notes that the build-up of a state inventory is associated with two major disadvantages: first, the government in reality does not have perfect foresight and therefore cannot determine the optimal extent of the stockpile; second, state demand for the inventory competes with private demand on the market, so it is possible that excess demand is exacerbated in the short run.

[14]A shifting of the tariff burden to the producers is highly improbable in the case of a quasi-monopoly.

3.2 The demand side

Following the analysis of supply-side attributes of the REE market, the demand side is now investigated. Before identifying the most important applications of REEs in the industry, the fundamental forces driving demand are considered.

3.2.1 Determinants of demand

There is widespread consensus in literature that demand for raw materials is determined by two forces: economic growth and technological progress. Global GDP recently grew by about 3.8% per year, mainly driven by the strong expansion of emerging markets like China. Economic growth is predominantly responsible for demand on the commodities market - i.e. the market for materials that are extracted in large amounts and are employed in a broad range of applications. The role of technological development is prevailing on markets of specialties whose worldwide annual production does not exceed several 1,000 t. REEs can be attributed to the second group (Angerer et al. 2009; EC 2010; Goonan 2011).

As a consequence, demand for REEs rose sharply during the last decades because many newly developed technologies rely on them. Especially during the last 10 years demand has tripled (Milmo 2010). Up to 2007, supply still exceeded demand. Yet in 2008, the REO consumption level of 129,000 t (Goonan 2011) could not be covered by current production any more (see Table 3.4), so existing stocks had to be resorted to.

Although REEs are necessary inputs to many technical applications, from the perspective of the individual producer they usually comprise only a tiny share of total material requirements. Hence, in overall cost calculations of assembling industries they represent a correspondingly small part, so it can be assumed that price elasticity of demand for REEs is relatively small (USDE 2010). The implications of this assumption will be discussed in Sections 3.3 and 3.4.

In order to determine whether market power also exists on the demand side, Figure 3.4 lists the main importing countries of REE products in 2008.[15] It can be seen that demand is more widely dispersed internationally than supply. Though there are a few major importers, they do not represent a significant market share for themselves, which becomes apparent when the data presented in the figure are related to total demand as given above. Neither can an outstanding concentration at the company level be noticed because of the wide range of different applications of REEs in miscellaneous industries, as shown subsequently.

---

[15]The USA denotes an exception since data were only available for 2007.

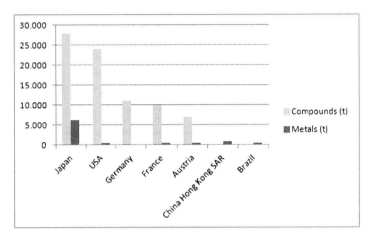

Figure 3.4: Demand for REE products by major importing countries. Source: compiled by the author, according to data from Walters and Lusty (2010).

3.2.2 Main applications of rare earth elements

Many industries compete for scarce raw materials (Angerer et al. 2009), and especially the clean energy sectors contribute to a large share of REE demand and are expected to grow even further in the future (USDE 2010). Table 3.5 gives an overview of the most relevant components manufactured from REEs and some examples of their applications.

In general, the industries reliant on REEs can be attributed to two groups: mature sectors - like catalysts, glassmaking, lighting, and metallurgy - and emerging sectors - including battery alloys, ceramics, and permanent magnets. Emerging markets still account for slightly less than half of REE demand, but it is noticeable that the largest share of consumption from these industries is driven by neodymium, praseodymium and dysprosium: the three elements together represent 85% of total REE demand from the emerging sectors (Goonan 2011).

Permanent magnets seem to be the most important individual component. They are employed in highly efficient electric motors and generators that power hybrid vehicles and e-vehicles, but are also used in renewable energy technologies such as wind turbines, small hydropower stations, or tidal power plants. Further possible applications are magnetic levitation trains, waste sorting, medical imaging techniques, and several IT technologies. Currently wind turbines are the most significant single field of permanent magnet application (Angerer et al. 2009; EC 2008; Goonan 2011; Hatch 2008).

Component	Applications	La	Ce	Pr	Nd	Pm	Sm	Eu	Gd	Tb	Dy	Ho	Er	Tm	Yb	Lu	Sc	Y
Permanent magnets	electric motors and generators, automated waste sorting, high-resolution diagnostic imaging techniques, miniaturised IT applications			x	x		x		x	x	x							
Phosphors	plasma displays, LCDs, energy-saving lamps, fluorescent lamps, radar equipment, cathode ray tubes	x	x	x	x			x	x	x			x					x
Catalysts	petroleum production, auto catalysts, chemical processing	x	x	x	x		x											
Glass industry	colouring, UV resistant glass	x	x		x													
Metallurgy and alloys	battery alloys, fuel cells, steel, aluminium/magnesium	x	x	x	x													x
Polish	polishing powders for TVs, computer monitors, mirrors, silicon chips	x	x	x	x													
Ceramics	colouring, stabilisation, capacitors, sensors, refractories	x	x	x	x			x	x		x					x		x

Table 3.5: Components, respective applications, and REEs employed for their production. Source: compiled by the author, according to data from Angerer et al. (2009); Cordier (2011b); EC (2008); Goonan (2011); Hatch (2008); Haxel et al. (2002); Liedtke and Elsner (2009); London (2010); USDE (2010); Walters and Lusty (2010).

Pr	Nd	Gd	Tb	Dy
70%	76%	69%	11%	100%

Table 3.6: Consumption of REEs in Nd-Fe-B permanent magnets as a share of total demand for the respective element. Source: compiled by the author, according to data from Goonan (2011). Data refer to 2008.

Permanent magnets nowadays are predominantly manufactured from neodymium, iron and boron (Nd-Fe-B) as this is the material yielding the strongest magnetic power. Nd-Fe-B magnets have widely crowded out samarium-cobalt magnets (Sm-Co) since the mid-1980s (Angerer et al. 2009). Sm-Co has been used since the 1970s because of its high efficiency and temperature stability, but regarding material costs it is not competitive with Nd-Fe-B (Kurronen et al. 2010; USDE 2010) as iron is much more abundant and therefore cheaper than cobalt. Moreover, magnetic power of Nd-Fe-B is up to 2.5 times higher (Walters and Lusty 2010) and remains stable for decades unless sudden temperature increases or corrosion occur. Meanwhile, solutions to overcome these vulnerabilities have been found: in humid environments, e.g. when applying permanent magnet technology to offshore wind power plants, surface coating of the magnets protects them from corrosion (Kurronen et al. 2010). For achieving an improved heat resistance, neodymium can be partially substituted by dysprosium (Cordier 2011b) or terbium (Kurronen et al. 2010) whereby 5 to 10% of neodymium content are replaced with one of the other materials. However, both additives belong to the REE group as well, with terbium being much scarcer and hence more expensive than many other REEs, including dysprosium; therefore terbium is rarely used as a permanent magnet supplement (London 2010; USDE 2010).

Another option is the use of didymium in magnets, a mixture of 75% neodymium and 25% praseodymium[16] (Cordier 2011b; London 2010). The 3:1 ratio is consistent with the natural abundance of the two elements and contributes to reduction of material costs as well as corrosion prevention (USDE 2010). Gadolinium plays only a minor role as a permanent magnet supplement (Goonan 2011).

Table 3.6 indicates that the permanent magnet sector demands large shares of total consumption of almost all of the REEs incorporated.[17] Especially demand for neodymium has risen sharply in recent years and has even outpaced supply (London 2010). Whereas permanent magnet production accounted for 55% of neodymium demand in 2006 (Angerer et al. 2009), its proportion had already reached 80% in 2009, out of which 10% were

---

[16] Praseodymium is generally employed as an additive or substitute in REE applications rather than a primary material (USDE 2010).

[17] Samarium demand has been omitted as Sm-Co magnets are hardly produced any more. Note that the table provides data with respect to permanent magnets, not to wind turbines that are one of their possible applications. A similar, but more extensive overview of end uses for REEs by amount of single REOs in all sectors can be found in Goonan (2011).

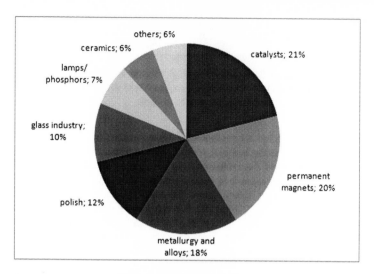

Figure 3.5: Share of REO consumption by major industries in 2008. Source: compiled by the author, according to data from Goonan (2011), Liedtke and Elsner (2009), London (2010) and Walters and Lusty (2010).

applied to wind turbines and hybrid vehicles (USDE 2010). Measured by value, magnets even represent 38% of REE consumption (Walters and Lusty 2010). In 2008, roughly 20% of total REO demand originated from the Nd-Fe-B magnet industry (Goonan 2011).

Figure 3.5 illustrates the relative importance of major industries for REO demand. In addition to the largest sectors named explicitly, the category "others" includes potential future markets like laser technology (Angerer et al. 2009; London 2010), hydrogen storage (Angerer et al. 2009), magnetic refrigeration (EC 2008; Haxel et al. 2002) and nanotechnology (EC 2008) that today only comprise a negligible share. Altogether, the sectors dependent on REE inputs are estimated to cover approximately 5% of global GDP (Milmo 2010). Yet, since many applications rely on the particular properties of certain single materials whose demand does not necessarily coincide with their natural abundance, supply-demand imbalances are prevailing on the REE market (Liedtke and Elsner 2009). The following section takes a closer look at the resulting price trends.

3.3 Price trends

Economic theory predicts that non-renewable natural resources are characterised by opportunity cost because once extracted and consumed, the resource is lost and cannot be used for another purpose any more. Therefore, the price of exhaustible resources reflects not only the marginal cost of extraction, but also has to cover opportunity cost. Hence, a smaller quantity is traded for a higher price than in the case of renewable resources, as Figure 3.6 illustrates for the static case. Considering a dynamic framework, the shadow price rises over time with the interest rate of the economy, a relation that is commonly referred to as the Hotelling rule (Wacker and Blank 1999). However, this theoretical setting only applies to perfectly competitive markets where agents have perfect foresight. In the following, the theoretical considerations are confronted with empirical data from the REE market to determine whether those assumptions are fulfilled here.

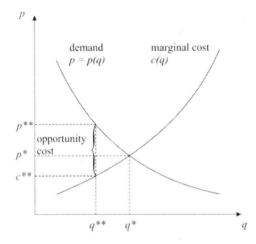

Figure 3.6: Pricing of a non-renewable resource. Source: Wacker and Blank (1999), modified by the author. Notation: q - quantity, p - price, c - marginal cost. Variables with an asterisk represent equilibrium values for renewable resources, those with two asterisks stand for the market outcome of non-renewable resources.

As Behrendt et al. (2007) point out, raw materials prices in general are highly volatile in the short and medium term. This may be due to supply-demand disequilibria that can either result in price fluctuations or quantitative shortages (USDE 2010). Several studies have empirically investigated the determinants of price development over time and come to the conclusion that production costs mark the lower limit (as predicted by economic theory) that is usually exceeded by internal influences and by external factors. Internal influences relate to effects on the raw material's own market such as changes in demand or supply patterns that yield imbalances, the occurrence of market power, scarcities, and prevailing expectations. These parameters mainly affect price development in the short run. External factors include geopolitical events, national policies like environmental legislation, economic growth, inflation or deflation, and natural disasters. The external determinants tend to induce rather long-term price developments. Regarding co- or by-production, the markets for minor products are usually more sensitive to shocks owing to close interrelationships with the major or co-products (Papp et al. 2008; USDE 2010; Walters and Lusty 2010).

Historically, nominal price development underwent several significant highs and lows that can be seen in Figure 3.7.[18] Starting with REE extraction on a commercial scale in the 1950s, prices fell after a peak in the mid-1950s until the early 1970s, mainly driven by the opening of Mountain Pass mine that represented a sudden positive supply shock. Subsequently, costs of production increased due to inflation and risen energy costs, resulting in higher REO prices. Yet in the early 1980s prices stabilised for a few years to rise again in 1985, induced by a decrease in demand that was answered by an even greater decrease in supply. In the 1990s, China considerably expanded its production (Walters and Lusty 2010) (see also Figure 3.3), thereby causing excess supply which led to lower price levels that are even estimated to be consistent with short-term marginal cost (USDE 2010). By the year 2000, the Nd-Fe-B magnet industry had acquired a significant impact, particularly driving demand for neodymium and dysprosium; when China - that had meanwhile become the major player on the market - reacted by expanding REE production, excess supply of other REEs that occurred as co-products was the consequence. In order to counteract price reductions, China restricted supply again, but did not succeed in guaranteeing high prices as at the same time REE demand from the IT sectors dropped, so supply still exceeded demand (Walters and Lusty 2010). Prices reached a trough in 2006, but since then have continuously increased until 2008. From 2007 on, Chinese domestic demand played an increasing role and export restrictions were introduced, contributing to rising prices as well (Papp et al. 2008). The following drop between 2008 and 2009 was due to the financial crisis that led industries to reduce their raw materials demand (EC 2008); the crisis was mainly perceptible in the automobile industry where demand for Nd-Fe-B magnets fell drastically, but recovered in the second half of 2009. As a consequence, sharp price increases have happened since 2009 (which is not visible in Figure 3.7 any more) (Cordier 2011a). In 2010 the prices of many individual REEs have escalated by 300 to 700% (USDE 2010); between October 2010 and July 2011 REO prices increased tenfold (Kern 2011). It is predicted that in the future excess demand will continue to prevail, bringing about further price rises. The EC (2008) refers to the REE market as underlying a super cycle.

---

[18]As mentioned earlier, data are usually provided for REOs which also applies for price information. REM prices closely follow the respective REO prices (USDE 2010).

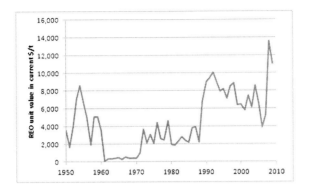

Figure 3.7: REO prices in current US dollars per metric ton from 1950 to 2009. Source: compiled by the author, according to data from Kelly and Matos (2010).

Papp et al. (2008) note that REO prices in the long run, when denoted in current US dollars - as in Figure 3.7 - closely follow inflation rates. Therefore an inflation-adjusted version is provided in Figure 3.8 with prices being normalised to 2008 levels. In contrast to the previous graph, the upward trend since the 1970s is not clearly visible any more. However, it is well-known from economic theory that the (inflation-adjusted) price of a non-renewable natural resource should rise over time to account for increasing scarcity (Tietenberg 2006). As this is not the case here, it can be concluded that owing to several disturbances on the REE market, prices are no reliable indicators of actual scarcity.[19]

All in all, shocks that were predominantly caused by technological change on the demand side and the emergence of market power on the supply side made the REE market pass from excess supply to a situation of excess demand. Total demand for REOs had risen by 46% in 2008 compared to 2003 (Walters and Lusty 2010) while export restrictions from China started to take effect and reduce the availability of raw materials.

Prices of individual REEs can vary considerably and do not necessarily follow the trajectories depicted for REEs as a whole; an example for the price development of selected REOs is given in Table 3.7.[20] As a general rule, heavy REEs are usually more expensive than their lighter counterparts (USDE 2010) which can be justified by their lower abundance (Walters and Lusty 2010). However, as light REEs also underly Chinese export restrictions, they have recently been subject to price increases as well (USDE 2010). Re-

---

[19]Rosenberg (1973) already discovered a similar pattern for several natural resources: he points out that despite remarkable fluctuations in the short run, the long-term price trend shows only a moderate upward slope.

[20]Yet in contrast to the downward price trend shown until mid-2009, prices have risen considerably since then (USDE 2010).

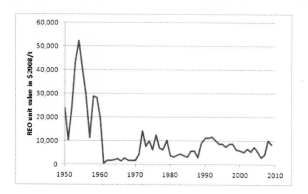

Figure 3.8: REO prices in 2008 US dollars per metric ton from 1950 to 2009. Source: compiled by the author, according to data from Kelly and Matos (2010).

garding rare earths used in wind turbine generators, the USDE (2010) study suggests that neodymium, dysprosium and terbium availability will be highly critical both in the short and medium term, whereas praseodymium and samarium are assessed to be uncritical. Data for gadolinium are not provided.

Yet for some REE consumers, current prices play only a subordinate role because they have signed long- or short-term agreements with resource producers, fixing the price in advance. Similar contracts exist on a bilateral level (Behrendt et al. 2007; USDE 2010). The tendency toward supply agreements results from the lack of stock exchange trading on the REE market (Liedtke and Elsner 2009). Instead, the role of an intermediary is often taken over by companies that specialise in raw materials trading (Walters and Lusty 2010). The absence of a freely adjusting market brings about weak and potentially unreliable price signals (USDE 2010).

Although the enormous short-run price swings that occurred in the last two to three years are not representative of the medium- to long-term market development, they can be explained by the previous statements that both REE supply and demand are characterised by low price elasticities: they imply a supply and demand curve with relatively steep slopes each, so exogenous shocks primarily yield price reactions and only minor quantity reactions. It is reasonable to assume that the low price elasticities hold for a short-term assessment whereas in the long run the market can adjust more easily, e.g. by the means discussed in Section 3.4, so the long-run price elasticities are higher, which justifies the moderate price development monitored over a longer time horizon.

To answer the question raised at the beginning of this section, the analysis has proven that the REE market cannot be considered a perfectly competitive market as assumed in

REO	Price June 2001	Price June 2002	Price June 2003	Price June 2004	Price June 2005	Price June 2006	Price June 2007	Price June 2008	Price June 2009
La	7.00	2.30	1.50	1.62	1.45	2.15	2.82	8.83	5.90
Ce	4.00	2.25	1.68	1.62	1.37	1.65	2.63	4.38	3.80
Nd	11.00	4.35	4.42	5.75	6.05	11.07	31.15	32.88	14.50
Pr	6.20	3.94	4.19	8.00	7.55	10.70	30.37	32.61	14.50
Sm	9.00	2.98	2.67	2.67	2.60	2.40	3.12	4.80	4.75
Dy	35.00	20.00	14.60	30.30	36.40	70.44	88.30	120.80	112.00
Eu	310.00	240.00	235.40	310.50	286.20	240.00	311.00	491.00	495.00
Tb	135.00	170.00	170.00	398.20	300.00	434.00	575.40	740.00	360.00

Table 3.7: REO prices for selected elements from 2001 to 2009. Source: Lynas (2010).
Prices refer to a minimum purity of 99%.

economic theory (USDE 2010). Instead, the price mechanism is disturbed by different
kinds of market failure and the existence of widespread longer-term price agreements.

3.4 Mitigation options for market imbalance

It has already been revealed that the REE market is currently characterised by a situation
of excess demand. This section investigates possibilities to potentially overcome the disequilibrium. The most frequently named measures are recycling and substitution of critical
materials[21] (Tietenberg 2006; USDE 2010).

However, excess demand is a quite recent phenomenon; until the mid-2000s, the REE
market was rather characterised by oversupply, so processing industries had little incentive
to pursue recycling or substitution (Walters and Lusty 2010). It remains to be seen whether
their efforts will now increase - this is not self-evident because of their low short-run
price elasticity of demand. Since research and development into mitigation options raise
additional costs, REE-consuming firms will only invest in them if they expect raw materials
prices to remain high in the longer term (USDE 2010) or if they are forced to find solutions
to sustained quantitative supply disruptions.

---

[21] Further options, like the discovery of new resources or efficiency increases due to technological progress,
are considered exogenous from the perspective of the individual firm and therefore remain unregarded
here. (Although companies can actively pursue research and development activities on their own, the
success of technological advancements is to a large part dependent on exogenous influences.)

3.4.1 Recycling

For an economy, waste products of non-renewable resources have two implications. On the one hand, environmental degradation causes welfare losses for the society. On the other hand, the waste may be recycled, i.e. used as a secondary resource stock, thus yielding a welfare gain (Wacker and Blank 1999). It is therefore utility-enhancing to pursue recycling as it can contribute to a reduction of negative externalities.

In detail, recycling has numerous advantages. First, it serves environmental preservation by lowering waste flows, being conducive to energy efficiency, and reducing air pollution, thereby abating climate change impacts (EC 2008, 2010; Kuhn et al. 2003). Second, it can substitute for primary raw materials (EC 2010), which can result in a restructuring of international resource markets if formerly import-dependent countries develop alternative ways to access raw materials and hence weaken the market power of primary resource suppliers (Kuhn et al. 2003). Third, as a consequence of the second point, the overall reserve base is expanded (Kuhn et al. 2003; Tietenberg 2006), an effect which Pittel et al. (2010) refer to as creating a "quasi-'renewability' of the resource stocks".

However, recycling faces several barriers to being widely implemented. First, in many countries practical hurdles prevent recycling: waste management and collection systems are inappropriate, so recycling would imply significant transaction costs; furthermore, reliable information regarding the quality of recycled materials is often lacking, so consumers tend to distrust them (EC 2008). In addition, newly developed technical applications often have a long lifespan, thereby creating a lag between resource demand and the availability of corresponding scrap materials (EC 2010). Second, the negative environmental impact of the recycling process, originating from the use of partially toxic chemicals, is a frequently named counter-argument (Wacker and Blank 1999). Third, Kuhn et al. (2003) remark that balanced sustainable growth imperatively requires a recycling rate of unity; yet the laws of thermodynamics signify that the physical theoretical upper limit is smaller because recycling involves losses (Tietenberg 2006), which is why it is sometimes called "downcycling". Economic activity without environmental damage is therefore infeasible (Wacker and Blank 1999).

The implications of recycling for resource stock development over time can be expressed as follows:

$$S_t = S_0 + S_0 a + S_0 a^2 + S_0 a^3 + \cdots, \qquad (3.1)$$

with S_0 denoting the original (primary) resource stock, a the recovery rate, and S_t the resource stock at time t that includes both primary and secondary materials. When considering an infinite time horizon, Equation 3.1 can be modified to

$$S_t = \frac{S_0}{1-a}. \qquad (3.2)$$

Both equations prove that only a recycling rate of 100%, i.e. $a = 1$, can provide an infinite resource flow over time. If this is not the case, as the laws of thermodynamics postulate, the secondary resource stock becomes infinitesimally small, resulting in a finite supply of overall resources (Tietenberg 2006).

Figure 3.9 illustrates how REE scrap is currently disposed of. Recycling comprises a fraction of 0%, hence sustainable utilisation is far from being practised today. Graedel (2011) confirms that the recycling rate of REEs as a whole is below 1%. The global average recycled content as a share of total input to metal production accounts for less than 1% for most REEs, but falls in the range between 1 and 10% for lanthanum, cerium, praseodymium, neodymium, gadolinium and dysprosium (Graedel 2011).

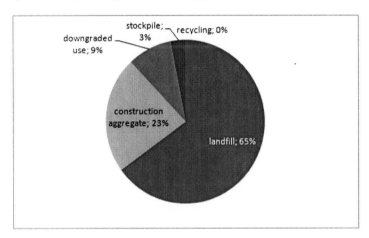

Figure 3.9: Current ways of REE disposal. Source: compiled by the author, according to data from Goonan (2011).

As for permanent magnets in particular, the feasibility of recycling has been demonstrated (Horikawa et al. 2006; Takeda et al. 2006), but the cost is still unknown (Jacobson and Delucchi 2011). Future prospects, e.g. by Angerer et al. (2009), appraise the recycling potential of Nd-Fe-B magnets to remain limited by 2030. Walters and Lusty (2010) point out that magnets produced from recycled materials may contain impurities and therefore provide an inferior performance. Additionally, another particularity of REEs impedes recycling. It is related to their dissipative use, which means that they occur in final products in very small concentrations and quantities (Behrendt et al. 2007). Consequently, the material is too widely dispersed to be economically collected in the first place, but even if it could be collected, an efficient recovery process would be infeasible under current conditions since large amounts of inputs, especially energy, are required to separate and regain the materials (Moriarty and Honnery 2011). Primary resource prices were quite low in the past, but if the price trend observed in the last three years is sustained or recycling technologies are improved, recovery of secondary resources will become economic as their value increases (Goonan 2011). However, this will only hold as long as the material intensity in final products remains unchanged; further miniaturisation and efficiency gains in applications will counteract this development by augmenting the effort of the recovery process (Moriarty and Honnery 2011).

A more probable alternative to conventional recycling is the reuse of permanent magnets. Owing to their decade-long lifespan without performance degradation, they can relatively easily be disassembled from disused applications and reintegrated elsewhere. Yet, if the magnets already suffer from corrosion or have been covered by plating materials that are unwanted in successive applications, the reuse may also be prohibitively expensive (Goonan 2011; Walters and Lusty 2010).

For many countries whose industries heavily rely on natural resource inputs, such as the EU member states, secondary materials are the only domestic possibility of resource supply (Angerer et al. 2009; EC 2008). Meanwhile it has become increasingly difficult for the EU to obtain scrap on the international secondary resource market. Whereas its imports of non-ferrous and precious metal waste fell by 40% between 2000 and 2008, exports rose by 125% during the same period, yielding shortages and price increases. This is due to scrap being illegally transported outside the EU rather than being recycled or reused domestically (EC 2008). Moreover, a level playing field on the global market for secondary raw materials is lacking: several non-EU countries raise export taxes, subsidise domestic waste treatment, or have implemented much less rigorous environmental directives (EC 2010).

As this section has shown, the incidence of REE recycling is currently negligible and is not expected to improve considerably in the near future. In the following it is analysed whether substitution possibilities allow for a more optimistic outlook.

3.4.2 Substitution

As indicated previously, REE demand in the short run is relatively inelastic owing to preexisting production technologies and equipment used in their processing. In the long run, however, these constraints lose importance, the modes of production are more variable, and the absolute value of price elasticity of demand increases. Hence, price changes have to be sustained to advance the adoption of substitutes (Tietenberg 2006). As in the case of recycling, the incentive for companies to substitute for REEs was rather limited so far since fierce price increases have only occurred during the last three years.

Generally, substitution is most efficient if it allows the replacement of a scarce and critical input with a more abundant material (EC 2010; Moriarty and Honnery 2011). Yet the applications employing REEs mostly rely on their specific properties (London 2010), so substitutes are either not available at all or they provide a lower-grade performance (Cordier 2011b). If there are substitutes for certain kinds of REEs, they often contain other REEs or even more critical materials (Walters and Lusty 2010).

Concerning permanent magnets in particular, a substitute for neodymium yielding comparable performance has not been discovered yet (Angerer et al. 2009) in spite of 20 years of scientific research on the issue (Walters and Lusty 2010). If neodymium became prohibitively expensive, the production of Sm-Co magnets could be resumed on a larger scale, but again efficiency losses would have to be accepted (Angerer et al. 2009). Moreover, although excess supply of samarium is predicted to sustain, guaranteeing comparably moderate prices, cobalt is usually considerably more expensive than the alloys used in Nd-Fe-B magnets. Since samarium also comprises only a small share of overall REE production (see Figure 3.2) and is hardly used for industrial purposes (see Table 3.5), it is unlikely to become a major driver of REE production (USDE 2010), so its supply is expected to depend on its co-products more strongly than in the case of neodymium, implying an even lower price elasticity of supply.

If substitution of REEs in the permanent magnet sector is difficult to achieve, their replacement in other sectors can be an option to mitigate overall demand. For example, lithium-ion batteries can be employed instead of nickel-metal-hydride batteries, thus decreasing the need for cerium, lanthanum and neodymium (Goonan 2011). Furthermore, in metallurgy, nuclear energy, hydrogen storage, glass polishing and ceramics there are viable alternatives to REE utilisation, but these only represent a small market share; most applications are expected to remain dependent on REEs (Walters and Lusty 2010).

Another possibility would be the substitution of other types of magnets for entire permanent magnets, first of all electromagnets. Their main weakness, though, is the much larger size, resulting in greater space requirement within the final application (Aston 2010). Morcos (2009) suggests the use of sintered ferrite permanent magnets that do not rely on REE inputs. Although they provide an inferior performance in wind turbines when it comes to low wind speeds, their component materials are more abundant and therefore lower-priced, so the return on investment for sintered ferrite permanent magnets is estimated to be equal or even slightly better than that of Nd-Fe-B magnets.

Finally, the replacement of permanent magnet generators in wind power plants with ceramic high-temperature superconductors is recommended.[22] However, they contain yttrium, another rare earth (USDE 2010), and therefore substitute one critical material for another, which may postpone the problem, but not solve it.

All in all, research is currently pursued in order to find materials that can either completely replace REEs or reduce the requirement for them, but significant progress is anticipated to take several years (Aston 2010). The only reasonable alternatives at the present time seem

---

[22]For ceramic superconductors, "high temperature" means that they can operate at up to -140°C.

to be the replacement of entire rare earth permanent magnets, especially with sintered ferrite permanent magnets (Morcos 2009), or REE substitution in other industries.

3.5 Consequences for future market development

The analysis in this chapter has shown that the REE market is highly complex and subject to many interrelations. Although the absolute abundance of REEs in the earth's crust turned out not to be that critical, the low concentrations in which they naturally occur impose severe restrictions upon economic production. Additionally, four kinds of market failure on the supply side complicate the situation: REEs are mined as by-products of other minerals, they are bound together as co-products, their mining and processing causes environmental damage, and China has quasi-monopolistic market power. The fact that almost half of current worldwide reserves is concentrated in China points to the probably persistent nature of its position, but also reveals the existence of alternative mining locations to be developed in the future.

Regarding the demand side, REEs are classified as specialty materials rather than commodities, which implies that the need for them is predominantly driven by technological progress. Recently many new applications requiring REEs as inputs have emerged or are at present being investigated. One of the most important applications of REEs is their use in permanent magnets that are, inter alia, employed in wind turbines.

The combination of supply restrictions and increasing utilisation of REEs in the industry yields supply-demand imbalances that have led to drastic price increases, especially in the last three years. However, as far as the long-term price trends are concerned, an increase that exceeds inflation rates could not be observed. This contradicts economic theory as depletable natural resources should face rising prices over time to account for increasing scarcity. It can thus be concluded that the prices witnessed at the market do not reflect actual scarcities, but are disturbed by the market failure described above and the prevalence of price agreements.

To mitigate current shortages and price fluctuations, recycling and substitution options of REEs have been examined. Recycling is hardly being pursued today and faces obstacles indicating that it will only become economic in the case of persistently high prices for primary resources. From a present-day perspective, reuse of permanent magnets appears to be more viable than conventional recycling. As for substitution, a replacement of REEs within permanent magnets is not possible so far if efficiency is supposed to be maintained. Instead, substitution of less critical materials for REEs is feasible in some other sectors, which could also contribute to excess demand mitigation. Alternatively, magnet concepts without REE inputs can be adapted, apparently the most realistic option in the short and medium term.

Now the question arises how the REE market will continue to develop in the future. A look at the literature reveals that the trend toward rising demand is commonly believed to prevail. For example, Milmo (2010) estimates total rare earth demand to amount to 200,000 t per year by 2014, up from 129,000 t in 2008 (Goonan 2011), which is the most recent historical value available. The most important applications are expected to be automotive catalytic converters, permanent magnets, rechargeable batteries and lamps, altogether demanding especially large amounts of high-purity REE products. For permanent magnets in particular, the compound annual growth rate is anticipated to account for 8 to 15% in the same time horizon (Cordier 2011a,b; Liedtke and Elsner 2009; Walters and Lusty 2010).

A frequently used indicator for expressing the expected future natural resource demand from emerging technologies is its share of current worldwide resource production (Angerer et al. 2009; EC 2010). Values for neodymium range from 1.66 (EC 2010) to 3.82 (Angerer et al. 2009) in 2030. These figures have to be interpreted as follows: if yearly neodymium production remains unchanged, i.e. at current levels, by 2030,[23] demand from emerging technology sectors will exceed supply by a factor of 1.66 (or 3.82, respectively). For comparison, in 2006 the indicator constituted 0.23 (EC 2010) or 0.55 (Angerer et al. 2009), respectively.[24] Even though the magnitude of the indicator differs among the sources, the principal statement that demand from emerging technologies will substantially rise remains valid.[25] Moreover, at the present time there are no phase-out technologies foreseeable that rely on neodymium (Angerer et al. 2009).

Concerning the materials employed in wind turbine generators, only praseodymium and samarium are assessed to be sufficient in the short to medium term. Neodymium, dysprosium and terbium shortages are already perceptible today and they are expected to persist. This prospect once more emphasizes the need for alternatives or material intensity improvements with regard to Nd-Fe-B permanent magnets (USDE 2010).

In general, it takes 5 to 10 years for newly designed technologies to mature while the time lag between the planning of new mining projects and their start of production ranges from 5 to 15 years (Behrendt et al. 2007; London 2010; Milmo 2010; USDE 2010). This means that supply adjustment can theoretically keep pace with changing demand-side patterns if technological developments can be anticipated (Behrendt et al. 2007), which does not seem to be the case in practice. The reasons for the considerable time lag between the identification of mineable deposits and their exploitation are various. They include difficulties with raising investment capital (EC 2008) - sometimes a mining company must even manage

---

[23] This is a highly improbable assumption, but it is necessary to ensure comparability of different points of time.

[24] As 2006 is taken as a base year in both references, "current production" in the fraction's denominator also refers to the value from 2006.

[25] It is remarkable that despite the data from both sources differ considerably, they are both consistent with the EC (2010)'s prediction that neodymium demand from emerging technologies will rise to 700% of current levels by 2030.

to find potential purchasers for the mine's output and bind them contractually before production can actually start (USDE 2010). Besides, planning and legal permit phases vary depending on the location, but can take several years. In some cases the existing infrastructure is not sufficient and has to be expanded first. Further possible bottlenecks are delays in equipment delivery or a lack of skilled staff (EC 2008). Finally, overall experience with REE mining projects is quite limited outside China (London 2010).

In spite of these barriers, global expenditure for the exploration of new mines has continuously increased since 2002 (EC 2008). In order to reduce their import dependency, many countries now pursue their own REE mining projects. In the USA the reopening of Mountain Pass is currently being planned. In Australia the Mount Weld deposit is being prepared for REE production (Angerer et al. 2009). Further locations anticipated to start REE mining in the next years include Canada, Malawi (Cordier 2011b), India (Liedtke and Elsner 2009), Vietnam (USDE 2010), South Africa, Greenland, Kyrgyzstan, and Namibia (Walters and Lusty 2010). A gradual diversification of supply can therefore be expected by the end of this decade, although REO reserves at most sites and hence their REE production potential are relatively small compared to Chinese conditions. Moreover, the circumstances of REE production are more favourable in China than in other places, especially regarding competitiveness, as the processing of deposits there is associated with particularly low costs. Out of the alternative deposits listed here, Mountain Pass is the only location mined exclusively for REEs. The other sites target different ores as main products and process REEs as by-products only (Haxel et al. 2002; Walters and Lusty 2010). All these factors contribute to the appraisal that China's market power will probably be reduced to a small extent, but it will nevertheless retain a dominating position in the medium term.

Nonetheless, it is still beneficial for mitigation of excess demand to search for alternative mineral sources because further options, like substitution, recycling, efficiency increases, or intelligent demand management, will take years to develop and implement (Aston 2010; EC 2010). Meanwhile, REE mining outside China will become more economic if continued REE production and export restrictions as well as rising domestic demand within China yield further price increases on the world market (Cordier 2011a).

Regarding future pricing, it is anticipated that long-term agreements will lose their importance due to rising uncertainty resulting from more volatile currency and energy cost developments. Outstandingly high prices are expected for materials that are demanded by emerging technology industries and whose supply is already beginning to show tightness, predominantly neodymium, dysprosium, terbium, yttrium and europium (London 2010; Walters and Lusty 2010).

When switching to a long-term assessment, uncertainty becomes even more apparent. Since market power, its influences on international trade, and resulting price volatility are rather short- to medium-term phenomena, REE criticality can then be evaluated by reserve availability (although this concept also involves several weaknesses, as described earlier in this chapter) (Behrendt et al. 2007). The fact that this indicator did not point to the occurrence of scarcity in the past does not justify the assumption that this will remain valid in the future (Tietenberg 2006). However, reserve figures are not the only data sources to rely on: developments of geopolitics and economic circumstances are equally important (EC 2010). These trends are even more difficult to predict, but play a crucial role, e.g. when policies target the deployment of clean energy technologies and thus induce a positive shock on REE demand (USDE 2010). The relevance and possible directions of policy interventions can also be retraced in Figure 3.10, which additionally provides a graphic summary of this chapter, illustrating the supply chain of critical materials with its associated problems and potential solutions.

As a result from the analysis conducted so far, it can be concluded that REE shortages and further price increases are likely to occur, but accurate predictions are impossible (USDE 2010). However, the consequences of further wind power deployment for REE demand have not been investigated up to now. Hence, Chapter 4 analyses possible pathways and their respective implications.

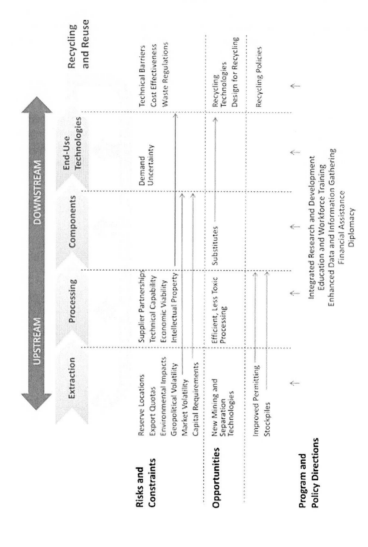

Figure 3.10: Supply chain of critical materials. Source: USDE (2010).

4 Estimates for future rare earth requirements from wind power deployment

Definite predictions of the future market development are obviously impossible owing to several factors that cause uncertainty, such as reserve disposability, potential political constraints, or data availability in general. Still policymakers and economic agents rely on future prospects for the design of their strategies. There are basically four ways to cope with this problem (Moriarty and Honnery 2011). First, econometric forecasting is the easiest method: by identifying certain empirical patterns in the past, it is stated that they are representative of the further trend as well. However, this method is prone to failure if a longer time horizon is to be assessed or structural changes are likely to occur, thus inhibiting the continuation of past trends. Second, some researchers count on expert surveys like the well-known Delphi analysis. Third, in the case of a highly uncertain situation associated with substantial risk, an application of the precautionary principle is often recommended, although it does not serve actual projection purposes. Finally, a scenario analysis is a very popular method especially in environmental and resource economics as it allows for the consideration of multiple plausible pathways. Yet it is important to bear in mind that the scenarios are not forecasts as such, but rather describe probable consequences subject to the corresponding assumptions (Martinot et al. 2007).

In this chapter, the precautionary principle is taken as a starting point for determining the upper and lower bound of rare earth demand from the wind power industry. A simplified approach is chosen to identify the actual magnitude of the problem. The following chapter lays the foundations for a scenario analysis based on the numerical model ReMIND-R that can be used to derive more accurate conclusions.

4.1 Methodology and assumptions

By means of a spreadsheet analysis, the extreme values of rare earth demand expected from wind energy deployment are assessed. In detail, a pathway for wind power deployment until 2050 is taken from literature. Herein the share of permanent magnet generators is varied according to estimates about their potential distribution, and respective consequences for REE demand from the wind industry are then derived and evaluated.

4.1.1 The choice of an appropriate indicator

For assessing natural resource scarcity, five indicators exist, one of them being defined physically as the reserve-to-use ratio, and the other four referring to economic measures (Tietenberg 2006). Each of them brings about its own advantages and disadvantages that are presented in Table 4.1.[1]

Eventually, none of them is irrevocably superior to the others. Owing to restricted data availability, the use of the scarcity rent, real marginal extraction cost, and marginal exploration and discovery cost turns out to be impracticable. As for real market prices, Chapter 3.3 showed that they underlie many distortions and hence are not compatible with the predictions of economic theory. Although the physical scarcity indicator, as introduced in Chapter 3.5, also has considerable drawbacks, it appears most adequate for the presentation of the results of the boundary analysis.

4.1.2 A pathway for wind power deployment

Literature offers a wide variety of scenarios for the future deployment of renewable energy sources. They differ not only with respect to their assumptions about parameters and exogenous variables, such as demographic development, GDP growth, degree of policy action, prospective fuel and carbon prices, cost reduction achievements over time, and aggregate energy demand. They can also be classified as either descriptive or normative. In the former case, a value-free "if-then" investigation is conducted whereas in the latter case a certain target, e.g. for CO_2 reduction, is taken as the starting point from which possible mitigation paths are deduced. Unfortunately not all studies make their methodology sufficiently transparent to be unambiguously assigned to one of the two groups (Martinot et al. 2007).

Scenarios are commonly classified according to their underlying assumptions and most studies use a similar pattern, distinguishing between a reference and one or more advanced scenarios. The reference scenario, sometimes also called baseline, makes the most conservative assumptions regarding the implementation of policy measures, usually restricting further policy action to pre-existing agreements. Moreover, projected price increases of fuels and carbon are rather moderate and the corresponding renunciation of fossil fuels proceeds slowly. Advanced scenarios, often sub-divided into a medium and high scenario, presume more ambitious mitigation efforts in terms of policy action, significant technological progress in the renewable energy sector and steeper price increases of fuels and carbon, resulting in a faster spreading of renewable energy sources (GWEC and Greenpeace 2010; Martinot et al. 2007).

---

[1] More extensive explanations of the keywords given in the table can be found directly in the corresponding references.

Indicator	Advantages	Disadvantages
Physical		
Reserve-to-use ratio	• easy to calculate	• implies homogeneous quality of natural resource • reserve measure underlies uncertainty • does not account for stock augmentation
Economic		
Real market prices	• data readily available • forward-looking measure	• contain distortions: e.g. government intervention, lack of perfect foresight, no consideration of externalities • sensitivity to deflator choice
Scarcity rent (net price)	• forward-looking measure	• slope of marginal extraction cost curve must be known • not directly observable
Real marginal extraction cost	• allows for technological change	• no foresight • rare public information • no environmental costs included
Marginal exploration and discovery cost	• rising discovery costs over time point to increasing scarcity • principally observable	• rare public information

Table 4.1: Advantages and disadvantages of scarcity indicators. Source: compiled by the author, according to Perman et al. (2010) and Tietenberg (2006).

Among recent examples of studies covering the future of the global energy sector, the *Energy Technology Perspectives* (OECD and IEA 2010a) belong to the most prominent and frequently cited analyses, providing an extensive enquiry of the sector until 2050. Equally important is the *World Energy Outlook* (OECD and IEA 2010b), yet the current edition's time horizon ends already in 2035.[2] For wind power in particular, the *Global Wind Energy Outlook* by GWEC and Greenpeace (2010) is one of the most extensive studies reaching until 2050. There are many more pathways to be found, published by official institutions and organisations, interest groups and industry associations. As it is not trivial to select an adequate scenario to rely on in this thesis, comparative studies have also been considered to determine the range of existing estimates and identify a narrower interval that seems to reflect some kind of compromise among scientists.

One of the most suitable references for such a comparison appears to be the IPCC's *Special Report on Renewable Energy Sources and Climate Change Mitigation (SRREN)*, especially the chapter on wind power by Wiser et al. (2011). They investigate 152 long-term wind energy deployment scenarios from literature and rank their results to obtain a median value as well as a 25th to 75th percentile range across all studies. The indicators assessed in the *SRREN* are the global primary energy supply of wind energy (in EJ/yr) and wind energy's share in total global electricity supply (in %). The median values of the projections for 2050 range from 16 EJ/yr in the baseline case to 23 and 27 EJ/yr in the medium and high scenario, respectively.[3] These figures represent 9, 14 and 13% of total electricity supply in 2050 for each of the scenarios. The 25th to 75th percentile includes a range of primary energy supply between 14 and 44 EJ/yr (equivalent to 3,900 and 12,200 TWh/yr) across all scenarios.

The second comparative research paper to be examined is by Martinot et al. (2007) who conducted a survey of 17 global renewable energy studies. Although the most recent ones are not included due to the year of publication, their choice contains the most prominent and comprehensive works. The indicators referred to are primary energy from renewables and electricity provided by renewables, in agreement with the *SRREN*. The authors do not calculate median values, but present the full range of results. Across all scenarios, projected primary energy supply of renewable sources in 2050 ranges between 70 and 450 EJ/yr, representing a 10-15% share of total primary energy in the reference case, 25-30% in the medium and even 40-50% in the high scenarios. Electricity generation from renewable sources in 2050 accounts for 7,200-37,000 TWh/yr or 15-25% of total electricity production in the baseline case, 30-40% in the medium case, and 50-80% in the high scenarios. For wind power a wide range of results arises, varying between 2,400 TWh/yr (equivalent to 8% of worldwide power generation) and 7,900 TWh/yr (34%) in 2050. These latter fig-

---

[2]Owing to the restricted time frame, the *World Energy Outlook* has been excluded from the following comparison.

[3]For comparison with results from other sources, the primary energy supply of wind power is also reported in TWh/yr, yielding figures of 4,400, 6,500 and 7,600 TWh/yr, respectively.

Study	Primary energy production (EJ/yr)	Share of total electricity production (%)	Cumulative capacity (GW)	Average annual capacity addition (GW/yr)
Wiser et al. (2011)	16-27	9-14	-	-
Martinot et al. (2007)	9-28	8-34	-	-
OECD and IEA (2010a)	18	12	2,000	62.4
GWEC and Greenpeace (2010)	8-37	6-33	880-4,028	18-94

Table 4.2: Outcomes of different studies for the role of wind power in 2050. Source: compiled by the author.

ures overlap with the 25th to 75th percentile values given in Wiser et al. (2011), but appear to be more conservative altogether.

However, the data provided by Wiser et al. (2011) and Martinot et al. (2007) are not sufficient for the analysis of material requirements proposed in this thesis as no information about the deployment of wind turbines (in GW) is available and material intensities are always given in mass per capacity (e.g. kg/kW). Therefore, it is necessary to choose one of the individual studies as a reference. Table 4.2 presents the available options in a comparable way.[4]

With respect to the purpose of this first estimate, it appears most appropriate to choose a rather optimistic projection for wind power development because conservative estimates would result in a possible underestimation of rare earth requirements. However, the GWEC and Greenpeace (2010) study provides only fragmentary data on annual capacity additions; they are given in five-year intervals, but both growth rates and absolute extension seem to change each single year. Owing to the uncertainty associated with this lack of information, that study is refrained from in favour of the OECD and IEA (2010a) BLUE Map scenario. Underlying assumptions are as follows:

---

[4]Wind power's shares of total electricity production are given in the table for completeness, but cannot be compared across studies as each one relies on different assumptions concerning demand-side developments and respective total electricity generation. Lower bounds refer to baseline scenario results, whereas upper bounds represent high scenarios. In the case of the OECD and IEA (2010a) study, the unmodified BLUE Map scenario has been used as it is the only version for which detailed information on capacity deployment is provided. The capacity additions given for GWEC and Greenpeace (2010) do not include repowering; furthermore, actual growth as assumed in the study differs from this figure and changes over time, but for comparison with the OECD and IEA (2010a) study it has been converted to an average value. 48 GW/yr of total annual capacity addition as given by OECD and IEA (2010a) is allotted to onshore, and the remaining 14.4 GW/yr to offshore.

- World population will be 9,150 million by 2050.

- Global annual GDP growth is assumed to average 3.1%; in detail, it accounts for 3.3% from 2007 to 2015, 3.0% from 2015 to 2030, and 2.6% from 2030 to 2050.

- Energy prices in 2050 are expected as follows (all values in 2008 US dollars):

    - IEA crude oil imports: $70/barrel

    - natural gas imports: $7.9-9.7/MBtu[5]

    - OECD steam coal imports: $58/t

- The CO_2 price, which equals the marginal cost of CO_2 abatement, will amount to $175/t CO_2. If it is taken into consideration, the effective oil price reaches approximately $140/barrel in real terms.

- The BLUE Map scenario assumes efficiency increases, power sector measures, and widespread implementation of new technology options in order to achieve a halving of worldwide energy-related CO_2 emissions by 2050, compared to 2007 levels. As it has a pre-defined target, it can be classified as a normative scenario.

- The bottom-up partial equilibrium model IEA ETP covers 15 world regions. Its objective is to achieve the CO_2 reduction target at least cost.

- The demand side is represented by supplementary models based on an assumed energy efficiency improvement of 1.5% per year.

4.1.3 Technological progress expectations for wind turbines

Beyond the selection of a basic wind power deployment study, the following drivers are most relevant for the analysis pursued in this thesis: first, the distinction between onshore and offshore wind power plays a crucial role since the two concepts demand different technological specifications. Second, technology trends in general determine material requirements. Third, the impacts of efficiency increases, including the so-called "repowering", have to be considered. Hence, those points are discussed in the following in order to specify and justify the further assumptions.

---

[5]Million British thermal units; equivalent to $8.3-10.2/GJ.

The onshore-offshore ratio.   In 2010 the globally installed offshore capacity was about 3.1 GW and represented a 1.6% share of total wind power capacity, which amounted to 197 GW. In terms of capacity additions, 1,162 MW of new offshore plants accounted for 3.1% of total new installations, which amounted to 37,642 MW (WWEA 2011). As the disposability of adequate onshore sites becomes increasingly limited, the share of offshore installations is expected to rise considerably in the future (REN21 2010). Studies projecting the development of renewable energy supply consistently support this statement: suggested shares of offshore in total wind power capacity range from 15 to 24% in 2035, reaching even 18 to 32% in 2050 (Wiser et al. 2011). Concordantly the OECD and IEA (2010a) expect the proportion of new offshore installations to reach on average 23% by 2050.[6] The authors conclude that about one-third of total wind energy generation will originate from offshore plants by 2050.[7]

With regard to the technical potential of wind power, many papers affirm that no constraints due to limited availability of the wind resource, lack of suitable locations, or technical barriers exist. For the placement of the technical potential within the scheme of renewable energy potentials consider Figure 4.1. For the further assessment the technical potential has been chosen as a reference because it is the most frequently cited measure in literature.

Table 4.3 illustrates that estimates of the global technical potential of wind power vary widely. Nevertheless, the figures still exceed even the most optimistic assessments for wind power generation by 2050. The 75th percentile projected by Wiser et al. (2011) for 2050, 44 EJ/yr or 12,200 TWh/yr, is significantly lower than any of the technical potential limits. Even if the highest projection out of all 152 scenarios is taken into account, claiming 113 EJ/yr (31,400 TWh/yr) by 2050, the majority of technical potential analyses still ascertain no constraints. Hence, it is improbable that the global technical potential for wind energy will restrict its expansion in the foreseeable future. Moreover, future estimates of the technical potential are expected to yield even larger numbers than those given here as technological progress is advancing and current technical limits vanish (WBGU 2011).

Study	Onshore (EJ/yr)	Offshore (EJ/yr)	Total (EJ/yr)
Krewitt et al. (2009)	379	57.4	436.4
WBGU (2011)	-	-	1,700
Arvizu et al. (2011)	70-450	15-130	85-580

Table 4.3: Range of global technical potential estimates for 2050. For simplicity figures are only reported in EJ/yr. Source: compiled by the author.

---

[6]This fraction is derived from the yearly capacity additions as given above and therefore refers to rated capacity installed rather than the number of new turbines.

[7]The higher ratio of offshore in electricity generation compared to its share of installed capacity results from its higher yield.

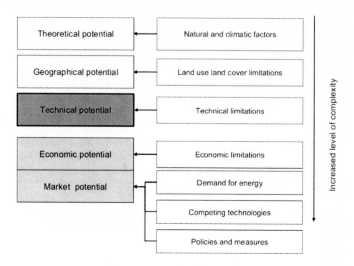

Figure 4.1: Scheme of renewable energy potentials with their corresponding influencing factors. Source: Krewitt et al. (2009).

A look at the projections for onshore and offshore wind energy generation in 2050 given by the OECD and IEA (2010a) BLUE Map scenario that is used in the further analysis reveals that both the total of 18 EJ/yr and the individual figures of 12 EJ/yr for onshore and 6 EJ/yr for offshore electricity production lie well below the technical potential frontier as indicated in Table 4.3 and can therefore be applied without causing difficulty in this respect.

Permanent magnet penetration.   General trends concerning the technological development of wind power plants include the increasing penetration of larger turbines that could be observed in the past (Hatch 2008; REN21 2010). Whereas the growth of onshore turbines may reach an upper boundary soon, such a limit is currently not predicted for offshore turbines (Wiser et al. 2011). As weight issues and reliability become more and more important with increasing turbine size and especially for offshore applications, gearless concepts will gain an increasing share of newly installed wind power plants, many of which will employ permanent magnet generators (EWEA 2009; Hatch 2008; REN21 2010; Wiser et al. 2011).[8] Wiser et al. (2011) estimate that improved drive train concepts have the poten-

---

[8]For completeness it should be mentioned that permanent magnet generators are not exclusively used in gearless designs (see Figure 2.2), but as the omission of the gearbox constitutes an advantage, their share in wind power plants with gearboxes is negligible.

tial to augment annual energy production of wind turbines by 4% while reducing turbine investment cost by 6%. Thus it appears reasonable to expect the current share of wind turbines operating with permanent magnet generators - about 10% - to rise during the coming decades (REN21 2010; USDE 2010). In accordance with the USDE (2010) study, the minimum penetration of permanent magnet technology by 2050 is assumed to remain at 10% for both onshore and offshore turbines, and the maximum is assumed to be 25% in onshore and 75% in offshore applications. Higher proportions do not seem to be realistic (Morcos 2009).

Recently, completely revised concepts for the utilisation of wind energy have been proposed, for example the vertical alignment of rotors in wind turbines that could also employ permanent magnet generators (Hatch 2008). However, the feasibility of those plans has not been demonstrated yet and some scientists doubt that the idea will ever become commercial (Lohse 2011a; Windkraft-Journal.de 2011). Due to the high uncertainty associated with those revolutionary concepts, they are not considered here.

Efficiency increases.   Finally, prospects for efficiency increases have to be regarded. Current state-of-the-art wind power plants can already operate near the theoretical maximum of aerodynamic efficiency as defined by the Lanchester-Betz limit: capacity factors of about 50% are not far from being achieved under ideal conditions (Wiser et al. 2011).[9] The potential for further improvement is therefore existent, but limited. Though in practice the performance of wind turbines varies strongly depending on wind availability at the respective site, so in the OECD and IEA (2010a) study a capacity factor of 28.6% is projected for 2050, representing a moderate improvement from today's 24.9%.[10] Since further innovation is mainly required to achieve a higher energy yield at locations with low wind speeds (OECD and IEA 2010a), permanent magnet synchronous generators may also be applicable there (see Figure 2.3).

Yet, today's wind turbines are already much more efficient and have a higher nominal capacity than those constructed 15 to 20 years ago (Hennicke et al. 2010). Since wind power deployment on a commercial scale started in the early 1990s (Bilgili et al. 2011) and wind turbines usually are assigned a lifetime of 20 years, the first cases of replacement now occur. As time proceeds, this phenomenon will become increasingly important. The replacement of many small turbines with a few large ones is called repowering; it can

---

[9]Remember that the Lanchester-Betz limit was 59.3%.

[10]Capacity factors have been calculated as follows: the 159 GW of capacity installed in 2009 could have provided 159 GW · 365 d/yr · 24 h/d = 1,393 TWh/yr if the capacity factor was 100%, but in effect only 347 TWh/yr have been produced by wind power in 2009 (GWEC and Greenpeace 2010), which is a proportion of 24.9%. Analogously the 2,000 GW predicted for 2050 by OECD and IEA (2010a) could provide 2,000 GW · 365 d/yr · 24 h/d = 17,520 TWh/yr, equivalent to 63 EJ/yr, but are expected to produce only 18 EJ/yr, a proportion of 28.6%. It has to be kept in mind that these figures refer to an "average" wind turbine and in reality differ with respect to the specific technology applied.

result in technological advantages and economic benefits (Bade et al. 2010) as modern wind power plants yield more full load hours and hence generate more electricity than their precursors. Due to lower maintenance efforts, overall costs of electricity generation decrease. Furthermore, grid compatibility has meanwhile improved and social acceptance of the new turbines is likely to rise because of lower noise levels (BWE 2010) and the fact that fewer wind power plants constitute an amelioration of the landscape's appearance (Heier 2009). The effect of repowering has already been accounted for in the OECD and IEA (2010a) study and therefore does not require additional attention with regard to the subsequent analysis.[11]

Another aspect of efficiency to be considered is related to the manufacturing stage of wind turbines. Here, the remaining potential for efficiency increases is vast, mainly with re-spect to material intensities. As mentioned previously, rare earth materials within wind turbines currently constitute between 0.2 and 3.3 t/MW. To obtain the projected material intensity in 2050, it is assumed that the lower end of this range, 0.2 t/MW, is retained. An even lower intensity is imaginable, but again with regard to the purpose of the thesis it seems to be more appropriate to overestimate rare earth requirements than to underestimate them. As for the magnet composition, a uniform mixture of 71.25% neodymium, 25% praseodymium and 3.75% dysprosium is assumed to constitute the rare earth content. This ratio results from the fact that didymium, which consists of three-quarters neodymium and one-quarter praseodymium, entails lower cost and improved corrosion prevention com-pared to pure neodymium; moreover, dysprosium is assumed to replace 5% of the remain-ing neodymium content to provide for better heat resistance. Thus the "optimal" permanent magnet composition is assumed to be generally applied. Sm-Co magnets are not consid-ered due to the negligible fraction they represent today. Gadolinium and terbium could in principle also be used in Nd-Fe-B magnets, but in practice they play a minor role as they offer no particular benefits and are quite scarce.

These data are used to derive the consequences of rare earth demand originating from the wind power industry. Figure 4.2 summarises the methodology of this chapter.

---

[11]From the annual addition of 62.4 GW/yr to the 2007 baseline of 94 GW installed capacity (REN21 2010) it can be concluded that yearly capacity extension represents gross supplements rather than the net effect: without decommissioning of old power plants, cumulative capacity would equal almost 2,800 GW in 2050. The IEA confirms that repowering has been considered, but is restricted to turbines that reach the end of their technical lifetime; earlier replacement for efficiency reasons is not assumed to occur (Remme 2011).

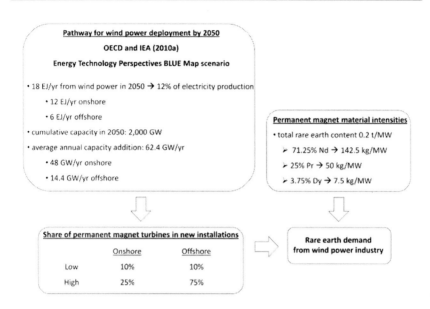

Figure 4.2: Methodology of the boundary analysis. Source: compiled by the author.

4.2 Results

Application of that methodology and assumptions yields the following demand projections for rare earths originating from the wind power sector (see also Figure 4.3): neodymium requirements range from 889.2 to 3,249.0 t/yr, praseodymium demand will be between 312.0 and 1,140.0 t/yr, and 46.8 to 171.0 t/yr of dysprosium will be needed. For comparison, in 2010 the annual wind power capacity addition totalled 37,642 MW/yr (WWEA 2011); assuming a 10% share of permanent magnet turbines for both onshore and offshore purposes, 536.4 t/yr of neodymium, 188.2 t/yr of praseodymium and 28.2 t/yr of dysprosium have approximately been consumed by the wind industry.

Over the entire time horizon from 2011 to 2050, a cumulative amount of 35,568 to 129,960 t neodymium, 12,480 to 45,600 t praseodymium and 1,872 to 6,840 t dysprosium will be employed in the low and high scenario, respectively, adding up to total rare earth demand of about 50,000 to 180,000 t (see Figure 4.4). Relative to current overall REO reserves of 88,000,000 t (see Table 3.2), those amounts equate to 0.06 to 0.20%. These percentages do not point to anticipated shortages per se, although a comprehensive assessment would

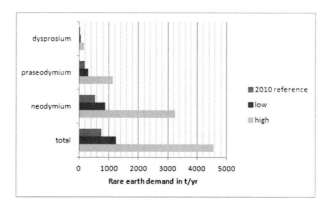

Figure 4.3: Demand projections for 2050 for the low and high permanent magnet penetration scenario. Source: compiled by the author.

also have to incorporate demand from the other industries, which is beyond the scope of this thesis.

For a relative consideration, the results depicted in Figure 4.3 can also be confronted with the scarcity indicator introduced in Chapter 3. It states what percentage of current production would have to be employed to meet future rare earth demand from the wind power industry and is calculated as follows:

$$J = \frac{D_{2050}}{P_{2010}},$$

with J denoting the scarcity indicator, D_{2050} refers to rare earth demand from the wind power sector projected for 2050, and P_{2010} is global rare earth production in 2010. Inserting the respective values for the three elements used in the assumed ideal permanent magnet yields[12]

$$J_{Nd,low} = \frac{889.2 \text{ t/yr}}{134,000 \text{ t} \cdot 0.159} = 4.2\% \text{ for neodymium,}$$

$$J_{Pr,low} = \frac{312.0 \text{ t/yr}}{134,000 \text{ t} \cdot 0.047} = 5.0\% \text{ for praseodymium,}$$

$$J_{Dy,low} = \frac{46.8 \text{ t/yr}}{134,000 \text{ t} \cdot 0.010} = 3.5\% \text{ for dysprosium}$$

in the "low" permanent magnet penetration case. The "high" scenario gives

$$J_{Nd,high} = \frac{3,249.0 \text{ t/yr}}{134,000 \text{ t} \cdot 0.159} = 15.2\% \text{ for neodymium,}$$

---

[12] 2010 production levels are taken from Table 3.4 and Figure 3.2.

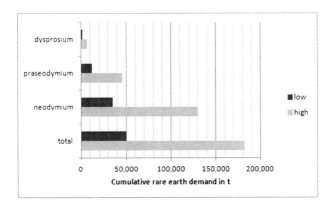

Figure 4.4: Cumulative rare earth demand from the wind power industry 2011-2050. Source: compiled by the author.

$$J_{Pr,high} = \frac{1,140.0 \text{ t/yr}}{134,000 \text{ t} \cdot 0.047} = 18.1\% \text{ for praseodymium},$$

$$J_{Dy,high} = \frac{171.0 \text{ t/yr}}{134,000 \text{ t} \cdot 0.010} = 12.8\% \text{ for dysprosium}.$$

It becomes apparent that the proportions rise considerably (see Figure 4.5): depending on the scenario, i.e. "low" or "high", 4.2 to 15.2% of 2010 neodymium production would have to be used in wind turbines by 2050, up from 2.5% in the base year. For praseodymium the figures reach 5.0 to 18.1%, up from 3.0% in 2010, and for dysprosium they amount to 3.5 to 12.8% as opposed to 2.1% in 2010. The wide ranges reflect the uncertainty associated with the analysis that becomes apparent in the choice of significantly varying permanent magnet penetration levels. Altogether, in the "low" scenario the ratios increase by 66% and in the "high" scenario they even rise by more than 500%.[13]

Although the analysis only includes rare earths' demand from the wind power industry, the sharp increases of the scarcity indicator imply that REE supply should rise during the next decades to ensure continuous provision of raw materials. As mentioned previously, rare earth requirements of other sectors are also likely to grow substantially, so even if current production levels still exceed projected rare earth demand from wind energy in 2050, they will not be sufficient for the overall economy.

---

[13] In an extreme scenario, Kleijn and Voet (2010) investigate material requirements for wind turbines under the assumption of a hydrogen economy in 2050 that is exclusively powered by renewable energy. They conclude that in the case of all offshore turbines being equipped with direct-drive permanent magnet generators, 180 times of 2008 neodymium mine production would be needed. Opposed to this result, the estimates given here under more realistic assumptions still appear very moderate.

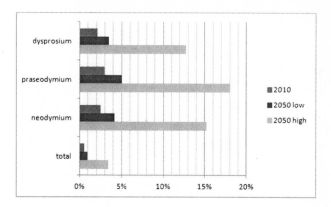

Figure 4.5: Ratio of rare earth demand from the wind power sector to 2010 production
levels. Source: compiled by the author.

As with every projection, it has to be kept in mind that the outcomes are subject to specific
assumptions, some of which may be challenged. First, the pathway chosen for future wind
power deployment represents a rather conservative estimate, but has been selected because
of relatively abundant data availability. Hence, the actual extension of the wind energy sector could yield faster capacity build-up than assumed. Second, annual capacity additions
are supposed to account for an average value that remains constant over time; however,
both absolute capacity additions and their share of pre-existing cumulative capacity have
always fluctuated historically. Owing to restricted data disposability, an average magnitude
has nevertheless been assumed. Therefore it is possible that rare earth demand exceeds the
figures presented here in some individual years, but falls below them in other years. Third,
the assumptions about material intensities are subject to uncertainty as well, but against
the background of available information are meant to be a "best estimate".

To summarise, the preceding analysis confirms claims from literature that present levels
of REE supply will presumably not be able to satisfy rising demand in the future. Potential mitigation options to rebalance supply and demand, such as material intensity improvements, diversification of suppliers, or recycling and substitution, have already been
discussed in detail in Chapter 3.

5 Application to ReMIND-R

In the previous chapter, a first estimate of the order of magnitude expected for future rare earth demand from wind power deployment was provided. Yet, a comprehensive assessment of rare earth scarcity actually requires the use of an integrated energy-economy-climate model. Such a model could also refine the enquiry by revealing concrete consequences for particular world regions within a dynamic framework. The selected model ReMIND-R has the additional advantage to cover a time horizon until 2100, thus allowing for the extension of the analysis to almost a century. As none of the established integrated assessment models already includes a rare earth constraint for renewable energy technologies, its implementation in the model code would exceed the scope of a master's thesis. Therefore, Chapter 5.2 merely offers two suggestions on how to account for the supply of rare earths and their demand by wind power generators. The result can be used by the modellers to realise the implementation. Chapter 5.1 lays the foundations for the subsequent section by giving an overview of the model structure.

5.1 The structure of ReMIND-R

This section contains a brief description of the main model features and relies on Leimbach et al. (2010) and Luderer et al. (2010). The most important equations are explained in Bauer et al. (2008). More detailed information can be found in these sources.

ReMIND is a model family and entails several versions. ReMIND-R, the version outlined here, covers the global scale in a regionalised form. ReMIND-G is also a global model, but forgoes the regional subdivision. Moreover, a model version specified to Germany, ReMIND-D, is currently being developed.

As a hybrid model, ReMIND-R combines the advantages of top-down and bottom-up models: it includes both the macroeconomic environment, thus facilitating policy analysis, and at the same time provides a detailed register of energy technologies. It consists of three interconnected modules: macro-economy, energy system, and climate. Model results are presented for 11 world regions.

Global population development is introduced as an exogenous scenario from the World Bank, reaching 9 billion by 2050 and 10 billion by 2100. The time horizon of the computations covers the period from 2005 to 2150 with a 5-year resolution; however, the model output is only reported up to the year 2100 to eliminate "apocalyptic" behaviour at the end of the time horizon.

ReMIND-R can be run in different modes. The "business as usual" case is the reference scenario, where optimisation is executed without any constraints. The "climate policy" case can be considered the advanced scenario; it incorporates a certain climate policy target that causes mitigation costs, thereby yielding a relative reduction of the net present value of welfare measures, like consumption or GDP.

In the following, the three modules are characterised in more detail. Figure 5.1 illustrates the main features and shows their interrelations.

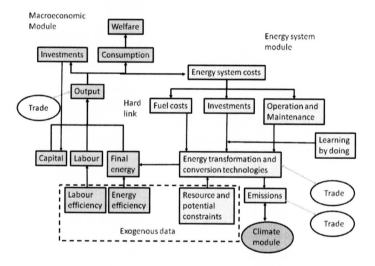

Figure 5.1: The structure of ReMIND-R. Source: compiled by the author, according to Leimbach et al. (2010).

5.1.1 The macroeconomic module

The macro-economy is modelled in a Ramsey-type way to maximise intertemporal welfare. The assumptions of perfect markets, perfect foresight and full cooperation ensure that the Pareto-optimal solution is concordant both with the global planner solution and with a cooperative solution. In the "climate policy" mode, the allocation of mitigation efforts is endogenous to guarantee a cost-efficient result.

Every world region is considered as a representative household whose utility depends upon consumption per capita:

$$U(r) = \sum_{t=t_0}^{T} \left(\Delta t \cdot e^{-\zeta(t-t_0)} L(t,r) \cdot \ln\left(\frac{C(t,r)}{L(t,r)}\right) \right) \quad \forall r, \qquad (5.1)$$

with $U(r)$ denoting the utility of the respective region, t is the time index, T symbolises the end of the time horizon, ζ is the pure rate of time preference assumed to equal 3%, L stands for population, and C is consumption. The intertemporal elasticity of substitution of per capita consumption is assumed to be 1.

All regional utility functions are aggregated to a global welfare function:

$$W = \sum_r (w(r) \cdot U(r)), \qquad (5.2)$$

where W represents global welfare and $w(r)$ are the weights attributed to the regions.[1]

As shown in Figure 5.1, GDP is generated from the production factors capital, labour and final energy. Production factors are combined via a constant elasticity of substitution (CES) function. Final energy is further subdivided into more specific types that are incorporated via a nested CES structure (see Figure 5.2).[2] The labour force is determined by exogenous data. The capital stock underlies depreciation at an annual rate of 5% and is augmented by investments.

GDP Y and final good net imports $M_G - X_G$ of a region have to cover all its expenditures, namely investments into the capital stock I, consumption C, and energy system costs. The latter are composed of fuel costs G_F, investments G_I, and operation and maintenance costs G_O. This results in the following budget constraint:

$$Y(t,r) - X_G(t,r) + M_G(t,r) \geq C(t,r) + I(t,r) + G_F(t,r) + G_I(t,r) + G_O(t,r) \quad \forall t,r. \quad (5.3)$$

Trade in ReMIND-R is based on the Heckscher-Ohlin and Ricardian models, i.e. it originates from different factor endowments and technologies across regions. Trade relations between individual regions are not modelled separately, but all exports and imports access one common pool. In addition to final goods, fossil primary energy carriers and emission permits can be traded.[3] On all three markets, a global trade balance must be sustained in

---

[1]The question how those weights are determined will be answered later in this section.

[2]Note that the elasticities of substitution σ in the figure should be given as decimal values, i.e. the commas must be read as decimal points.

[3]Emission permits are only traded in the "climate policy" scenario. For the initial allocation of CO_2 certificates, three different options have been assessed by Leimbach et al. (2010); however, as the second fundamental theorem of welfare economics suggests, they turned out to have no effect on the final outcome. If market imperfections are allowed for, the Coase theorem applies instead of the second fundamental theorem of welfare economics, but the implications remain the same.

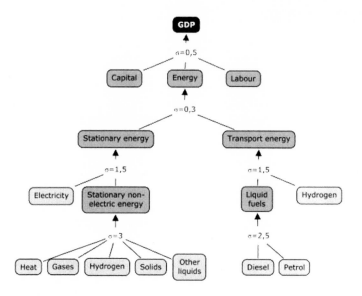

Figure 5.2: CES production structure in the macro-economy module. Source: Leimbach et al. (2010).

every single period:

$$\sum_r \left(X_j(t,r) - M_j(t,r) \right) = 0 \quad \forall t, j. \tag{5.4}$$

As before, X and M denote exports and imports, respectively. The index j is a placeholder for primary energy carriers E, the composite final good G and emission permits Q.

In the end, the possibilities of intertemporal trade and capital mobility induce a global equalisation of factor prices, resulting in an intertemporal and interregional equilibrium.

The intertemporal trade balance also plays a role in assigning the welfare weights $w(r)$ in Equation 5.2. They are adjusted by means of a Negishi procedure such that the sum of the discounted value of exports matches the sum of the discounted value of imports over the entire time horizon.

$$B^i(r) = \sum_t \sum_j \left(p_j^i(t) \cdot [X_j^i(t,r) - M_j^i(t,r)] \right) \quad \forall r, i, \tag{5.5}$$

$$w^{i+1}(r) = f(w^i, B^i(r)) \quad \forall r, i. \tag{5.6}$$

$B^i(r)$ represents the region's intertemporal trade balance at iteration step i and $p_j^i(t)$ symbolises the world market price of good j that corresponds to its shadow price obtained from Equation 5.4.

Equations 5.5 and 5.6 imply that a high intertemporal trade deficit, i.e. a low value of $B^i(r)$, reduces the welfare weight $w^{i+1}(r)$ of that region in the next iteration step. Consequently, global welfare is hardly raised by additional imports of the region, but rather benefits from its exports. The same reasoning applies in the other direction. As the objective is the maximisation of intertemporal welfare, regions will always approach an intertemporal trade balance of zero over time.

5.1.2 The energy system module

The energy system module is hard-linked to the macroeconomic module in two ways: first, as described above, GDP must cover all energy system expenditures. Second, final energy balance requires that final energy supply from the energy system module equals its demand as a production factor in the macroeconomic module. Thus, both modules are optimised conjointly.

The energy system can be interpreted as an economic sector with a heterogeneous capital stock, producing secondary and final energy carriers from primary energy carriers. Available primary energy carriers cover coal, oil, gas, uranium, hydro, wind, solar, geothermal, and biomass. Exhaustible resources, i.e. fossil fuels, uranium and biomass, face fuel costs that rise with increasing cumulative extraction. Since extraction costs differ across regions and exhaustible primary energy carriers are tradable, the optimisation calculus ensures that extraction from different deposits is conducted in least-cost order. Renewable energy sources are not affected by fuel costs, but their diffusion is restricted by exogenously given technical potentials. For onshore wind power, the technical potential is assumed at 120 EJ/yr, for offshore wind power at 40 EJ/yr.[4]

Primary energy carriers are transformed to secondary energy carriers by the use of 50 different conversion technologies. The resulting secondary energy carriers include all types that are depicted in orange boxes in Figure 5.2. Conversion technologies, usually power plants, are represented in the model via their capacities, whose build-up requires investments. Specific investment costs are determined endogenously for technologies that face learning-by-doing, which applies only to wind turbines and solar photovoltaics, and they are exogenous for all other technologies.

The primary energy carrier "wind" is exclusively converted to the secondary energy carrier "electricity" and underlies the following assumptions:

- Wind turbines are assigned a lifetime of 40 years.

- Investment costs are $1,200/kW.

---

[4]The distinction of onshore and offshore wind power is not modelled explicitly, so the technical potential is aggregated for wind power as a whole, with offshore being subject to a 50% investment cost penalty.

- A widespread deployment of wind turbines requires additional storage facilities due to the intermittent availability of wind power. This justifies an investment cost markup of 20% by 2050.

- Floor costs are $883/kW.

- The learning rate, i.e. the reduction of specific investment costs for each doubling of capacity, amounts to 12%.

- Cumulative capacity in 2005 is 60 GW.

- Operation and maintenance costs add up to $0.89/GJ.

Secondary to final energy conversion is modelled via transport and distribution capacities to the end users. The end use sectors households and industry are subsumed under the stationary sector. Furthermore, the transport sector demands final energy, as shown in Figure 5.2. Energy and CO_2 prices develop endogenously.

5.1.3 The climate module

The climate module is modelled in a rather simple way, containing an impulse-response function for the carbon cycle and an energy balance temperature model. It calculates the CO_2 concentration in the atmosphere and the consequences of greenhouse gas emissions and sulphate aerosols for global mean temperature. CO_2 is emitted in the course of primary to secondary energy conversion, specifically during fossil fuel combustion, but can be absorbed by carbon capture technologies. However, leakage can occur in the process of carbon capture and storage, thereby raising the level of CO_2 in the atmosphere. Other greenhouse gas emissions and CO_2 emissions originating from land use change are determined via marginal abatement cost curves or by assuming exogenous scenarios.

The climate sensitivity of ReMIND-R is fixed at 3.0°C. The introduction of climate policy targets is an additional constraint for welfare maximisation, but their achievement is facilitated by full intertemporal and interregional flexibility regarding mitigation efforts. Under a "climate policy" regime, CO_2 emissions from fossil fuel combustion have to be backed by emission permits that can either come from the stock originally allocated to the region or from imports.

5.2 Ways of implementing rare earth requirements of the wind power industry in ReMIND-R

As mentioned previously, ReMIND-R does currently not account for wind power deployment restrictions arising from the limited availability of REEs. One possibility for implementing this additional boundary is the introduction of fixed demand coefficients, a concept similar to the one presented in Chapter 4. However, this requires many exogenous assumptions. A more elaborate option is the explicit modelling of the REE market with endogenous price development. Both approaches are subsequently illustrated in a "cooking recipe"-like manner.

5.2.1 Fixed demand coefficients

Fixed demand coefficients would have to be implemented at the level of primary to secondary energy conversion technologies, at the conversion stage of the primary energy "wind" to the secondary energy "electricity" via wind power plants. This corresponds to the box "Energy transformation and conversion technologies" in Figure 5.1. Exogenous data should be added to the set of "Resource and potential constraints".

In general, two kinds of model input are necessary: the amount of rare earths available for the wind power sector - i.e. supply - and rare earth demand per GW of newly installed wind power capacity. As for the first aspect, the material limitation can either be introduced by providing the model with a fixed stock of rare earths, e.g. 5% or 10% of current reserves,[5] that can be freely distributed across the time horizon. Alternatively, in a more restrictive way, yearly rare earth supply can be predetermined in order to avoid the complete exhaustion of the available stock during the first few periods, as this is not compatible with today's mining infrastructure.

Concerning the demand side, onshore and offshore wind power have to be modelled as two separate technologies in ReMIND-R as they are very likely to differ according to rare earth demand. Such a distinction has not been explicitly included in the model yet. If the model is supposed to substitute autonomously among them, a further sub-distinction is necessary, introducing onshore and offshore wind power with and without permanent magnet generators each. All the technologies have to be provided with parameters for their respective efficiency, costs, etc., which poses a problem because data are difficult to obtain due to non-disclosure of wind turbine producers. If this challenge cannot be overcome, a more simple solution is to assume fixed shares of permanent magnet penetration. In this case, the distinction of two instead of four technologies is sufficient, limiting the complexity to

---

[5]The small share can be justified by the fact that rare earths are also needed as input materials in many other industries and cannot be employed exclusively for wind turbines.

an onshore and an offshore technology. Subsequently, the percentage of wind turbines operating with and without rare earth permanent magnets has to be defined. For example, the assumptions from Chapter 4 can be retained, implying that in a "low penetration" scenario 10% of both onshore and offshore plants use permanent magnet generators, whereas in a "high penetration" scenario the ratio is 25% for onshore and 75% for offshore installations. Finally, material intensities have to be assigned, stating what amount of REE inputs is required per GW of newly installed capacity.

The introduction of fixed shares allows for a simplified approach: it can be assumed that each wind turbine uses rare earths, but only 10% of the actual amount (in the "low penetration" scenario) and accordingly 25% (in the "high penetration" scenario for onshore) and 75% (in the "high penetration" scenario for offshore). The result would be the same as if only some turbines were assumed to use the "full" amount of rare earth inputs.

5.2.2 Modelling the REE market

The compilation of an REE market model is a more challenging option. Initially, the specific conceptual characteristics of rare earth demand and supply relevant for modelling have to be identified. As Chapter 3 revealed, the REE market is currently characterised by four kinds of market failure:

- By-production: REEs are usually not the primary target of mining, so price elasticity of supply is rather low.

- Co-production: REEs occur as compounds, which results in excess supply of some REEs and excess demand for others.

- Negative externality: extraction and processing cause environmental damage. Hence, without policy intervention, the price is suboptimally low and the quantity too high compared to a perfectly competitive market outcome without externalities.

- Market power: China acts as a quasi-monopolist, which yields a higher price and slower resource extraction than under perfect competition (Perman et al. 2010). To a certain extent, this effect may counteract the negative externality.

Moreover, at the demand side, rare earths usually constitute only a small share of total material requirements within their applications. This particularity, combined with the effect of production technology lock-in, contributes to a relatively low price elasticity of demand. However, this may only be true in the short run. Since the time horizon of ReMIND-R covers almost a century, long-term market structures are more relevant. As REEs become increasingly important for technological innovations, expected revenue may rise, so they may be extracted as primary products in the future, thus inhibiting the problem of by-production. Due to geological reasons, co-production cannot be overcome, and it is also highly uncertain whether current efforts to internalise the environmental burden will be sustained. Yet the impact of market power is likely to decline over time as REE reserves are widely distributed across the globe and the exploration of alternative mining locations is already under way. Furthermore, the potential for technological progress points to an increasing viability of economic extraction at sites outside of China and improved prospects of recycling and substitution options.

The REE market model should rather represent the probable long-term market structure than current conditions that can become redundant within the first few periods of the time horizon. Moreover, ReMIND-R is conceptualised as a social planner model. Consequently, the REE market model - as a "sub-model" incorporated into ReMIND-R - should follow the same approach to retain consistency. The chosen model framework therefore depicts the socially optimal resource extraction path over time and abstracts from presently prevailing market imperfections.[6]

The following information is needed for compiling the REE market model (Perman et al. 2010):

- REE demand function

- Hotelling's rule

- initial value of the natural resource stock, i.e. at $t = 0$

- final value of the natural resource stock, i.e. at $t = T$

To account for the demand side, the different wind power technologies must explicitly be modelled again, as in the case of fixed demand coefficients. Here it is sufficient to distinguish wind turbines with and without permanent magnets: the former are preferable due to their higher efficiency, but need rare earth inputs. The initial material intensity has to be given exogenously - e.g. 0.2 kg/kW - but may well be assumed to decline over time due to technological progress. Wind turbines without permanent magnets play the role of a backstop technology that is utilised if rare earths are either exhausted or reach a prohibitively high price level. As the model switches endogenously between the technologies, a further distinction of onshore and offshore wind power is not compulsory here, but may nevertheless add informative value if implemented.

As a tangible natural resource demand function, Perman et al. (2010) suggest the following form:

$$p(q) = Ke^{-bq}, \tag{5.7}$$

with p denoting price, q stands for the quantity of the natural resource extracted, and K and b are parameters. K is the choke price, which becomes clear if $q = 0$ is inserted in Equation 5.7. If the price level reaches the value of K, REE extraction stops, i.e. the intercept with

---

[6]Modifications of the basic model, e.g. to represent the case of a monopolistic market, can be found in Heijman (1991).

the price axis is reached, and the economy switches to the backstop technology. The demand function is depicted in the second quadrant of Figure 5.3.

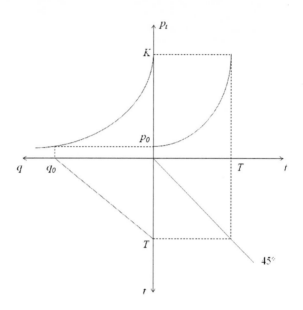

Figure 5.3: The social planner model of optimal resource extraction. Source: compiled by the author, according to Perman et al. (2010).

The intertemporal price path of the natural resource is shown in the first quadrant. It starts at p_0 and its slope can be derived from the Hotelling rule in the case of constant marginal extraction cost. The gross price then increases with the same rate as the net price, according to the rate of interest (which is assumed to equal the social discount rate):

$$p_t = p_0 e^{\rho t}, \tag{5.8}$$

where ρ represents the rate of interest.

The fourth quadrant merely displays a 45° line to copy the scale of the time axis. Finally, in the third quadrant, the natural resource depletion path is constructed. The straight line represents the resource depletion path over time, with q_0 indicating the quantity extracted at $t = 0$. The intercept with the resource extraction axis is determined by the quantity demanded for a price of p_0 (see the dashed lines). Resource depletion over time follows the path:

$$q_t = \frac{p}{b}(T - t). \tag{5.9}$$

The area below the curve corresponds to the total resource stock $\bar{S}$:

$$\int_0^T q_t dt = \bar{S}. \tag{5.10}$$

Efficiency requires that the resource stock is completely exhausted at the end of the time horizon, i.e. $S_T = 0$ and accordingly, $q_T = 0$. In the first quadrant, the choke price K is reached at $t = T$. That way it is guaranteed that the natural resource stock $\bar{S}$ is completely exhausted exactly when the switch to the backstop technology occurs. For the initial amount $S_0 = \bar{S}$ an exogenous value has to be defined.[7] When determining $\bar{S}$, it has to be kept in mind that wind power is not the only industry applying rare earths, so an adequate measure should only contain a certain percentage of the overall reserve base or identified resources.[8]

The implementation of the REE "sub-model" in ReMIND-R would have to be carried out as another "resource and potential constraint" for wind power in Figure 5.1. Yet in contrast to the pre-existing constraints, it does not only deliver exogenous data, but interacts with the wind power sector since the demand function for REEs is incorporated in the model, thus allowing for endogenous price development.

5.2.3 Evaluation of the two approaches

Expected results. The implementation of a rare earth restriction for wind power, irrespective of the concrete approach chosen, would result in a change of the wind power deployment pathway and, correspondingly, yield a different electricity mix. Via final energy supply and energy system costs, the macroeconomic module would be affected as well. If the restriction is binding, the model has to account for an additional constraint, thus the achievement of a first-best solution is precluded. Compared to the case without the rare earth restriction, the CO_2 target in the climate policy scenario can only be accomplished on a suboptimal path. Consequently, consumption losses and sequentially welfare losses are likely to increase.

---

[7]For simplicity, a fixed natural resource stock is assumed, although in reality new discoveries and technological progress continuously enlarge it.

[8]Reserve base or identified resources (see Figure 3.1) have been proposed as the underlying measure because over the time horizon of ReMIND-R, substantial technological progress can be expected, so current reserves do not appear appropriate. However, the final decision is up to the modellers.

	Assets	Drawbacks
Fixed demand coefficients	• simple and transparent	• exogenous assumption of fixed shares of permanent magnet penetration yields pre-determined outcomes (model artefact) • alternative introduction of separate wind power technologies with and without permanent magnets requires data that are difficult to obtain • estimate of available rare earth amount in a lump-sum way; reserves are a time-dependent measure
REE market model	• endogenous price development • endogenous choice of wind power technology	• data for implementation of wind power technologies with and without permanent magnets are difficult to obtain • choice of an adequate measure for the fixed natural resource stock is problematic

Table 5.1: Assets and drawbacks of the two approaches to implement a rare earth restriction in ReMIND-R. Source: compiled by the author.

Assets and drawbacks of both concepts. Table 5.1 summarises the main advantages and disadvantages of the two approaches presented in Sections 5.2.1 and 5.2.2. Although both concepts face several obstacles, the market model allows for more endogeneity and is therefore recommended for the implementation of a rare earth restriction in ReMIND-R due to its higher informative value.

However, the application of the standard natural resource extraction model to rare earths can be questioned. Up to now, literature has concentrated on hydrocarbons like coal, oil and natural gas, but in contrast to REEs, they occur in large concentrations at a few deposits. It has to be investigated if the different properties of REEs require the development of an own model or if minor adaptations of the existing approach are sufficient. For example, the assumption of constant marginal extraction cost appears to be too optimistic for REEs. One would rather expect rising marginal cost, which could easily be implemented in the REE market model by prescribing that the intertemporal price path proceeds steeper than predicted by the Hotelling rule. It is important to note that the Hotelling rule would still apply to the net price, i.e. the royalty, but as marginal extraction costs would then have a slope greater than zero, the gross price would grow at a larger rate than the net price. If an investigation of the applicability of the standard model to REEs reveals that minor adaptations are sufficient to account for their particularities, overall results will not change much. If this is not the case, a research gap will emerge, calling for a completely new modelling concept.

6 Conclusion

Wind power is often perceived as the most environmentally friendly (or "clean") renewable energy technology. However, most assessments do not account for the fact that critical natural resources are employed at the construction stage of wind turbines. Together with the globally soaring deployment of wind power, a potential problem arises that has received little attention in literature so far and has been examined in detail in this thesis.

In an initial step, critical natural resources that are relevant for wind power have been identified. "Criticality" is thereby characterised by high economic importance plus supply and/or environmental risk. Magnetic materials, particularly rare earths, have been determined as the most critical input materials to wind turbine construction and are therefore the core of this thesis. They are used in the range of 0.15-3.3 kg/kW of nominal capacity and are assembled in permanently excited synchronous generators. Compared to alternative generator models, this type benefits from reduced weight, higher efficiency, lower operation and maintenance efforts, and the eschewal of an external power source; yet, there is no possibility to influence its voltage, and materials for the construction of permanently excited synchronous generators are associated with high costs.

With respect to material requirements, onshore and offshore power plants mainly differ in their utilisation of bulk materials. Furthermore, low maintenance effort is of special interest for offshore applications, which makes direct-drive permanent magnet generators particularly attractive. Although permanently excited synchronous generators at present only cover a market share of about 10% in wind turbines, an increasing market share is expected in the future, partly driven by the expansion of the offshore segment.

Motivated by the definition of criticality, a market analysis of rare earth elements has been provided next, starting at the supply side. The Herfindahl-Hirschman Index of 0.23 does not point to a critical geographical reserve distribution per se. Still 97% of mine production are currently concentrated in China, which illustrates the first of four kinds of market failure on the REE market. The Chinese quasi-monopoly is facilitated by preferential natural resource endowment and low-cost production, but policy measures such as export tariffs and quotas caused the share of exports in overall Chinese REE production to drop to a quarter, which recently resulted in severe supply shortages for foreign industries. Besides the dominant position at the country level, market power also exists at the company level since a few large Chinese state corporations constitute the vast majority of suppliers on the world market. A second market imperfection arises due to the natural occurrence of REEs as co-products: REEs can only be mined in fixed composites that do not necessarily coincide with demand-side patterns, yielding excess demand for some individual REEs and excess supply for others. Third, REEs are by-products of more abundant minerals and are therefore subject to a low price elasticity of supply. Finally, their extraction and processing is responsible for environmental burdens, i.e. negative externalities.

Regarding demand-side features, REEs can be attributed to specialty materials rather than commodities, implying that demand for them is predominantly driven by technological development. They usually comprise only a small share of total material requirements within their applications, so price elasticity of demand can be considered relatively low, at least in the short run. Market power does not prevail at the demand side: an outstanding concentration of REE consumers can neither be observed at the country level nor at the company level. Among the various applications of REEs in the industry, permanent magnets are the most important individual component today, with wind turbines being the most significant single field of permanent magnet use.

As far as the pricing of depletable natural resources is concerned, a static and dynamic framework can be distinguished. At a certain point of time, the price is the sum of marginal extraction cost and opportunity cost. For price development over time, the Hotelling rule applies, stating that the shadow price of the natural resource rises with the interest rate. Yet, both theoretical concepts only apply to perfectly competitive markets. An investigation of empirical REO prices reveals, however, that those predictions do not hold for the data actually observed. This can be justified by the existence of distortions, e.g. the absence of a freely adjusting market and the prevalence of longer-term contracts, yielding unreliable price signals.

Two mitigation options for overcoming the disequilibrium on the REE market have been discussed. It became evident that recycling is not economic with the current state of technology and today's price levels; reuse of permanent magnets is a more promising alternative. The substitution of permanent magnets is principally possible, but a substitute that guarantees comparable performance to Nd-Fe-B magnets has not been discovered yet. As a consequence, the shortages and price increases are likely to persist in the short to medium term. Yet, the global distribution of reserves indicates that a dispersion of REE mining is feasible, but a considerable diversification of supply on the world market may require a few decades.

The market analysis has been followed by a first estimate of the REE demand pattern originating from new wind turbine installations by 2050. Based on the wind power deployment path from the IEA BLUE Map scenario, the order of magnitude has been determined by means of a spreadsheet analysis. Depending on the assumptions on permanent magnet penetration in newly installed wind turbines, rare earth requirements for wind turbines turned out to rise by 66 to 500% compared to their 2010 levels. As REE demand from other sectors is also expected to increase substantially, it could be concluded that the current level of supply is highly unlikely to be sufficient in the long run. However, geological scarcity of rare earths is not foreseeable.

For a more elaborate analysis of that problem, the utilisation of an integrated assessment model has been proposed. Therefore, ReMIND-R has been presented. It follows
an intertemporal welfare maximisation objective and consists of the three modules macro-
economy, energy system, and climate. Two ways have been suggested for implementing
a natural resource availability restriction to account for rare earth demand from the wind
power industry: the introduction of fixed demand coefficients, an approach similar to that
in the previous chapter, and the explicit modelling of the REE market. The implementation
of one of these proposals in the source code remains to be done by the modellers.

Altogether, it turns out that the problem examined in this thesis deserves more attention
since a supply bottleneck of REEs has the potential to impede wind power deployment,
thereby endangering an important aspect of climate change mitigation. As the development of new REE sources requires significant lead time, priority should be assigned to the
topic.

Moreover, some open questions remain for further research. First, the net external effect of
REEs should be determined, contrasting pollution due to the extraction and processing of
REEs and their contribution to energy-efficient and emission-reducing technologies. With
that information, adequate policy implications for dealing with the externalities could be
derived. Second, it has to be examined whether the standard natural resource depletion
model can be applied to REEs or if their particular properties require a new approach.
Third, a comprehensive assessment of rare earth restrictions in ReMIND-R requires an
investigation of all renewable power generation technologies that employ these materials.
The analysis could also be extended to other natural resources in the same framework.

Bibliography

Ackermann, Thomas and Lennart Söder (2002). "An overview of wind energy-status 2002". In: *Renewable & Sustainable Energy Reviews* 6, pp. 67–128.

Akhmatov, Vladislav et al. (2003). "Variable-speed wind turbines with multi-pole synchronous permanent magnet generators. Part I: Modelling in dynamic simulation tools". In: *Wind Engineering* 27.6, pp. 531–548.

Ancona, Dan and Jim McVeigh (2001). *Wind Turbine - Materials and Manufacturing Fact Sheet.* URL: http : / / www . perihq . com / documents / WindTurbine-MaterialsandManufacturing_FactSheet.pdf.

Angerer, Gerhard et al. (2009). *Schlussbericht Rohstoffe für Zukunftstechnologien. Einfluss des branchenspezifischen Rohstoffbedarfs in rohstoffintensiven Zukunftstechnologien auf die zukünftige Rohstoffnachfrage.* Tech. rep. IZT Institut für Zukunftsstudien und Technologiebewertung; Fraunhofer ISI Institut System- und Innovationsforschung.

Ardente, Fulvio et al. (2008). "Energy performances and life cycle assessment of an Italian wind farm". In: *Renewable & Sustainable Energy Reviews* 12.1, pp. 200–217.

Arvizu, D. et al. (2011). "IPCC Special Report on Renewable Energy Sources and Climate Change Mitigation". In: ed. by O. Edenhofer et al. Cambridge University Press. Chap. Technical Summary, pp. 34–212.

Aston, Adam (Oct. 2010). *China's Rare-Earth Monopoly.* URL: http : / / www . technologyreview.com/energy/26538/.

BMWi (Oct. 2010). *Rohstoffstrategie der Bundesregierung. Sicherung einer nachhaltigen Rohstoffversorgung Deutschlands mit nicht-energetischen mineralischen Rohstoffen.* Tech. rep. BMWi - Federal Ministry of Economics and Technology.

BWE (2010). *Repowering von Windenergieanlagen. Effizienz, Klimaschutz, regionale Wertschöpfung.*

— (2011). *Technik. Kapitel 5: Konstruktiver Aufbau einer Windkraftanlage.* BWE - Bundesverband Windenergie (German WindEnergy Association). URL: http://www.wind-energie.de/infocenter/technik.

Bade, P. et al. (2010). *Windkraftanlagen. Grundlagen, Entwurf, Planung und Betrieb.* Ed. by Robert Gasch and Jochen Twele. 6th ed. Vieweg + Teubner.

Bauer, Nico et al. (2008). *REMIND: The equations.* Tech. rep. PIK Potsdam Institute for Climate Impact Research.

Behrendt, Siegfried et al. (2007). *Seltene Metalle. Maßnahmen und Konzepte zur Lösung des Problems konfliktverschärfender Rohstoffausbeutung am Beispiel Coltan.* Tech. rep. Umweltbundesamt.

Bilgili, Mehmet et al. (2011). "Offshore wind power development in Europe and its comparison with onshore counterpart". In: *Renewable & Sustainable Energy Reviews* 15, pp. 905–915.

Bruckner, T. et al. (2011). "IPCC Special Report on Renewable Energy Sources and Climate Change Mitigation". In: ed. by O. Edenhofer et al. Cambridge University Press. Chap. Annex III: Cost Table, pp. 1485–1516.

Cordier, Daniel J. (July 2011a). *2009 Minerals Yearbook. Rare Earths [Advanced Release].* Tech. rep. U.S. Geological Survey. URL: http://minerals.usgs.gov/minerals/pubs/commodity/rare_earths/myb1-2009-raree.pdf.

— (Jan. 2011b). *Rare Earths.* Tech. rep. U.S. Geological Survey. URL: http://minerals.usgs.gov/minerals/pubs/commodity/rare_earths/mcs-2011-raree.pdf.

Dena (2011). *Turbinen der Multimegawattklasse.* dena - Deutsche Energie-Agentur (German Energy Agency). URL: http://www.offshore-wind.de/page/index.php?id=6336.

EC (2003). *External Costs. Research results on socio-environmental damages due to electricity and transport.* Tech. rep. European Commission.

— (2008). *The raw materials initiative - Meeting our critical needs for growth and jobs in Europe.* Tech. rep. Commission of the European Communities.

— (2010). *Critical raw materials for the EU. Report of the Ad-Hoc Working Group on defining critical raw materials.* Tech. rep. European Commission Enterprise and Industry, Fraunhofer ISI.

EWEA (2009). *Wind Energy - The Facts. A guide to the technology, economics and future of wind power.* Ed. by European Wind Energy Association. Earthscan.

Eerens, Hans and Ayla Uslu (2009). *Europe's onshore and offshore wind energy potential. An assessment of environmental and economic constraints.* Tech. rep. 6. EEA - European Environment Agency.

Ender, Carsten (2011). "Wind Energy Use in Germany - Status 31.12.2010". In: *DEWI Magazin* 38, pp. 36–48.

Enercon (2010). *ENERCON Windenergieanlagen. Technologie und Service.* Tech. rep. ENERCON GmbH.

Fingersh, L. et al. (Dec. 2006). *Wind Turbine Design Cost and Scaling Model.* Tech. rep. NREL/TP-500-40566. National Renewable Energy Laboratory, U.S. Department of Energy.

Fischedick, Manfred (2010). *Potenziell treibende Kräfte und potenzielle Barrieren für den Ausbau erneuerbarer Energien aus integrativer Sichtweise. Endbericht.* Tech. rep. Wuppertal Institute for Climate, Environment and Energy.

GWEC and Greenpeace (Oct. 2010). *Global wind energy outlook 2010.* Tech. rep. Global Wind Energy Council.

Goonan, Thomas G. (2011). *Rare Earth Elements - End Use and Recyclability.* Tech. rep. U.S. Geological Survey. URL: http://pubs.usgs.gov/sir/2011/5094/pdf/ sir2011-5094.pdf.

Graedel, T. E. (2011). *Recycling Rates of Metals - A Status Report.* Tech. rep. UNEP - United Nations Environment Programme. URL: http://www.unep.org/ resourcepanel/Portals/24102/PDFs/Metals_Recycling_Rates_110412-1.pdf.

Hatch, Gareth P. (May 2008). *Going Green: The Growing Role of Permanent Magnets in Renewable Energy Production and Environmental Protection.* Dexter Magnetic Technologies, Inc. URL: http://www.terramagnetica.com/papers/Hatch-Magnetics-2008.pdf.

— (Aug. 2009). *How Does The Use Of Permanent Magnets Make Wind Turbines More Reliable?* Terra Magnetica. URL: http://www.terramagnetica.com/2009/08/03/ how-does-using-permanent-magnets-make-wind-turbines-more-reliable/.

Hau, Erich (2008). *Windkraftanlagen. Grundlagen, Technik, Einsatz, Wirtschaftlich-keit.* Springer.

Haxel, Gordon B. et al. (2002). *Supporting Sound Management of Our Mineral Resources. Rare Earth Elements - Critical Resources for High Technology.* Tech. rep. U.S. Geological Survey. URL: http://pubs.usgs.gov/fs/2002/fs087-02/fs087-02.pdf.

Heier, Siegfried (2009). *Windkraftanlagen: Systemauslegung, Netzintegration und Regelung.* Ed. by Siegfried Heier. 5th ed. Vieweg + Teubner.

Heijman, W. J. M. (1991). *Depletable resources and the economy.* Ed. by J. A. Renkema et al. Wageningse Economische Studies 21. Landbouwuniversiteit Wageningen.

Hein, Matthias von (Sept. 2010). *China verknappt High-Tech-Rohstoff: Das gute Geschäft mit den seltenen Erden.* URL: http://www.tagesschau.de/wirtschaft/china1056. html.

Hennicke, Peter et al. (2010). *EnergieREVOLUTION. Effizienzsteigerung und erneuerbare Energien als globale Herausforderung.* Ed. by Peter Hennicke and Susanne Bodach. oekom.

Herbert, G. M. Joselin et al. (2007). "A review of wind energy technologies". In: *Renewable & Sustainable Energy Reviews* 11, pp. 1117–1145.

Horikawa, Takashi et al. (2006). "Effective recycling for Nd-Fe-B sintered magnet scraps". In: *Journal of Alloys and Compounds* 408-412, pp. 1386–1390.

Jacobson, Mark Z. (2009). "Review of solutions to global warming, air pollution, and energy security". In: *Energy & Environmental Science* 2, pp. 148–173.

Jacobson, Mark Z. and Mark A. Delucchi (2011). "Providing all global energy with wind, water, and solar power, Part I: Technologies, energy resources, quantities and areas of infrastructure, and materials". In: *Energy Policy* 39, pp. 1154–1169.

Kelly, Thomas D. and Grecia R. Matos (Nov. 2010). *Historical Statistics for Mineral and Material Commodities in the United States. U.S. Geological Survey Data Series 140*. U.S. Geological Survey. URL: http://minerals.usgs.gov/ds/2005/140/.

Kern, Joachim (Aug. 2011). *Neues Recyclingverfahren für Seltene Erden*. CleanEnergy-Project. URL: http://www.cleanenergy-project.de/17827/.

Kleijn, Rene and Ester van der Voet (2010). "Resource constraints in a hydrogen economy based on renewable energy sources: An exploration". In: *Renewable and Sustainable Energy Reviews* 14, pp. 2784–2795.

Krewitt, Wolfram et al. (2009). *Role and Potential of Renewable Energy and Energy Efficiency for Global Energy Supply*. Tech. rep. Umweltbundesamt.

Kuhn, Thomas et al. (2003). "Recycling for sustainability - a long run perspective?" In: *International Journal of Global Environmental Issues* 3.3, pp. 339–355.

Kurronen, Panu et al. (2010). *Challenges in applying permanent magnet (PM) technology to wind power generators*. URL: http://www.theswitch.com/files/2010/05/EWEC-2010_Paper_Challenges-in-applying-PM-technology_Panu-Kurronen-The-Switch_final-2.0_100417.pdf.

Leão, R. P. S. et al. (2007). "An Overview on the Integration of Large-Scale Wind Power Into the Electric Power System". In: *International Conference on Renewable Energies and Power Quality*.

Leimbach, Marian et al. (2010). "Mitigation Costs in a Globalized World: Climate Policy Analysis with REMIND-R". In: *Environmental Modeling and Assessment* 15, pp. 155–173.

Liedtke, Maren and Harald Elsner (Nov. 2009). *Seltene Erden*. Commodity Top News 31. BGR Bundesanstalt für Geowissenschaften und Rohstoffe (Federal Institute for Geosciences and Natural Resources). URL: http://www.bgr.bund.de/cln_109/nn_323580/DE/Gemeinsames/Produkte/Downloads/Commodity__Top__News/Rohstoffwirtschaft/31__erden,templateId=raw,property=publicationFile.pdf/31_erden.pdf.

Lohse, Jenny (July 2011a). *US-Studie empfiehlt Einsatz vertikaler Rotoren in Windparks*. CleanEnergy-Project. URL: http://www.cleanenergy-project.de/17689/.

— (May 2011b). *Umweltschäden durch Neodym in der Windkraft*. CleanEnergy-Project. URL: http://www.cleanenergy-project.de/16734/.

London, Ian M. (2010). *The Delicate Supply Balance and Growing Demand for Rare Earths*. URL: http://avalonraremetals.com/_resources/IL_010.01_Magnetics.pdf.

Luderer, Gunnar et al. (2010). *Description of the ReMIND-R model*. Tech. rep. PIK Potsdam Institute for Climate Impact Research.

Lynas (2010). *Annual Report 2009*. Tech. rep. Lynas Corporation Ltd. URL: http://www.lynascorp.com/content/upload/files/Reports/Annual_Report_2009_778195.pdf.

Martinot, Eric et al. (2007). "Renewable Energy Futures: Targets, Scenarios, and Pathways". In: *Annual Review of Environment and Resources* 32, pp. 205–239.

Martínez, E. et al. (2009). "Life cycle assessment of a multi-megawatt wind turbine". In: *Renewable Energy* 34.3, pp. 667–673.

Milmo, Cahal (Jan. 2010). *Concern as China clamps down on rare earth exports*. The Independent. URL: http://www.independent.co.uk/news/world/asia/concern-as-china-clamps-down-on-rare-earth-exports-1855387.html.

Morcos, Tony (2009). "Harvesting Wind Power With (or Without) Permanent Magnets". In: *Magnetics Business & Technology* 8.2, p. 26.

Moriarty, Patrick and Damon Honnery (2011). *Rise and Fall of the Carbon Civilisation. Resolving Global Environmental and Resource Problems*. Ed. by Patrick Moriarty and Damon Honnery. Springer.

Musgrove, Peter (2010). *Wind Power*. Ed. by Peter Musgrove. Cambridge University Press.

NYSERDA (2005). *Wind Turbine Technology Overview*. Global Energy Concepts. URL: http://www.powernaturally.org/programs/wind/toolkit/9_windturbinetech.pdf.

Neumann, Thomas et al. (Nov. 2002). *Weiterer Ausbau der Windenergienutzung im Hinblick auf den Klimaschutz - Teil 2*. Tech. rep. BMU - Federal Ministry for the Environment, Nature Conservation and Nuclear Safety.

OECD and IEA (2010a). *Energy Technology Perspectives 2010 - Scenarios & Strategies to 2050*. Ed. by OECD and IEA. Organization for Economic Cooperation & Development.

— (2010b). *World Energy Outlook 2010*. Ed. by OECD and IEA. International Energy Agency.

Papp, John F. et al. (2008). *Factors that influence the price of Al, Cd, Co, Cu, Fe, Ni, Pb, Rare Earth Elements, and Zn*. Tech. rep. U.S. Geological Survey. URL: http://pubs.usgs.gov/of/2008/1356/pdf/ofr2008-1356.pdf.

Perman, Roger et al. (2010). *Natural Resource and Environmental Economics*. Ed. by Roger Perman et al. 3rd ed. Pearson.

Pittel, Karen et al. (2010). "Recycling under a material balance constraint". In: *Resource and Energy Economics* 32, pp. 379–394.

REN21 (2010). *Renewables 2010 Global Status Report*. Tech. rep. GTZ Deutsche Gesellschaft für Technische Zusammenarbeit.

Rehfeldt, Knud et al. (2001). *Weiterer Ausbau der Windenergienutzung im Hinblick auf den Klimaschutz - Teil 1*. Tech. rep. BMU - Federal Ministry for the Environment, Nature Conservation and Nuclear Safety.

Remme, Uwe (Nov. 2011). Personal communication.

Rogner, H.-H. (1997). "An assessment of world hydrocarbon resources". In: *Annual Review of Energy and the Environment* 22, pp. 217–262.

Rosenau-Tornow, Dirk et al. (2009). "Assessing the long-term supply risks for mineral raw materials - a combined evaluation of past and future trends". In: *Resources Policy* 34.4, pp. 161–175.

Rosenberg, Nathan (1973). "Innovative responses to materials shortages". In: *American Economic Review* 63.2, pp. 111–118.

Schleisner, L. (2000). "Life cycle assessment of a wind farm and related externalities". In: *Renewable Energy* 20, pp. 279–288.

Tagesschau (Nov. 2010a). *Berichte über weitere Rohstoffverknappung: China will seltene Metalle noch seltener machen*. URL: http://www.tagesschau.de/wirtschaft/rohstoff102.html.

— (Dec. 2010b). *Exportzölle steigen: China verteuert Ausfuhr Seltener Erden*. URL: http://www.tagesschau.de/wirtschaft/selteneerden102.html.

— (Jan. 2011a). *Deutschland-Besuch von Vize-Premier Li: Bundesregierung fordert Zugang zu Chinas Rohstoffen*. URL: http://www.tagesschau.de/wirtschaft/china1150.html.

— (July 2011b). *Studie japanischer Wissenschaftler: Riesige Vorkommen Seltener Erden entdeckt*. URL: http://www.tagesschau.de/wirtschaft/selteneerden104.html.

Takeda, Osamu et al. (2006). "Recovery of neodymium from a mixture of magnet scrap and other scrap". In: *Journal of Alloys and Compounds* 408-412, pp. 387–390.

The World Bank Group (2011a). *Worldwide Governance Indicators - One Indicator for Selected Countries*. URL: http://info.worldbank.org/governance/wgi/mc_chart.asp.

— (2011b). *Worldwide Governance Indicators - World Map*. URL: http://info.worldbank.org/governance/wgi/worldmap.asp.

Tietenberg, Thomas H. (2006). *Environmental and natural resource economics*. Ed. by Thomas H. Tietenberg. 7th ed. Addison-Wesley.

Tour, Arnaud de la et al. (2011). "Innovation and international technology transfer: The case of the Chinese photovoltaic industry". In: *Energy Policy* 39, pp. 761–770.

Tryfonidou, Rodoula and Herrman-Josef Wagner (n.d.). *Kurzfassung: Offshore-Windkraft. Technikauswahl und aggregierte Ergebnisdarstellung.* Tech. rep. Ruhr-Universität Bochum.

USDE (2010). *Critical Materials Strategy.* Tech. rep. U.S. Department of Energy.

WBGU (2011). *World in Transition - A Social Contract for Sustainability.* Tech. rep. WBGU - German Advisory Council on Global Change. URL: http://www.wbgu.de/fileadmin/templates/dateien/veroeffentlichungen/hauptgutachten/jg2011/wbgu_jg2011_en.pdf.

WWEA (2006). *Wind Energy - Technology and Planning.* World Wind Energy Association. URL: http://www.wwindea.org/technology/ch01/estructura-en.htm.

— (Apr. 2011). *World Wind Energy Report 2010.* Tech. rep. World Wind Energy Association. URL: http://www.wwindea.org/home/images/stories/pdfs/worldwindenergyreport2010_s.pdf.

Wacker, Holger and Jürgen E. Blank (1999). *Ressourcenökonomik. Band II: Erschöpfbare natürliche Ressourcen.* Ed. by Artur Woll. Wolls Lehr- und Handbücher der Wirtschafts- und Sozialwissenschaften. R. Oldenbourg.

Walters, Abigail and Paul Lusty (2010). *Rare Earth Elements.* British Geological Survey, Natural Environment Research Council. URL: http://www.bgs.ac.uk/downloads/start.cfm?id=1638.

Weinzettel, Jan et al. (2009). "Life cycle assessment of a floating offshore wind turbine". In: *Renewable Energy* 34.3, pp. 742–747.

Windkraft-Journal.de (July 2011). *Für Windparks sind Vertikalturbinen bis zu 10 mal effektiver.* URL: http://www.windkraft-journal.de/2011/07/17/fur-windparks-sind-vertikalturbinen-bis-zu-10-mal-effektiver/.

Wiser, R. et al. (2011). "IPCC Special Report on Renewable Energy Sources and Climate Change Mitigation". In: ed. by O. Edenhofer et al. Cambridge University Press. Chap. Wind Energy, pp. 755–863.

Yale University and Columbia University (2011). *Country Scores.* Yale Center for Environmental Law & Policy, Center for International Earth Science Information Network. URL: http://epi.yale.edu/Countries.

CPSIA information can be obtained at www.ICGtesting.com
Printed in the USA
LVOW08s1616070214

372818LV00002B/292/P

9 783658 049126